TABLE

Begun on Feb 12- 2006

finished June 3 2007

The beginning of the gospel about Jesus Christ,
the Son of God (1:1).

— 1 —

The Beginning of the Gospel
Mark 1

DIMENSION ONE:
WHAT DOES THE BIBLE SAY?

Answer these questions by reading Mark 1

1. What is the task of the messenger as the prophet describes it? (1:2-3)

   To prepare the way of the Lord and make his paths straight

2. What is the main message of John the Baptist? (1:4, 7)

   He preached the baptism of repentance for the remission of sins and There cometh one mightier then I after me, The latchet of whose shoes I am not worthy to stoop down and unloose. I baptised with water, He will baptise you with the Holy Ghost

3. What clothing does John the Baptist wear? (1:6)

   Camel hair and a girdle of a skin

4. What food does he eat? (1:6)

   Locusts and wild honey

5. What is the first event in the life of Jesus that Mark records? (1:9)

He was baptized by John in the Jordan River

6. How does the Spirit appear on this occasion? (1:10)

like a dove descending upon Him

7. What does the voice from heaven say? (1:11)

"Thou art my beloved Son, in whom I am well pleased."

8. Where does Jesus go after this event? (1:12-13)

He went into the wilderness for forty days

9. What is the first message of Jesus according to Mark? (1:14-15)

He came into Galilee, preaching the Gospel of the Kingdom of God. Saying the time of God is at hand; Repent ye, and believe the gospel

10. To whom does Jesus extend his invitation by the Sea of Galilee? (1:16, 19)

Simon Peter, and Andrew his brother and James and John his brother son of Zebedee

11. What is the first invitation Jesus extends? (1:17)

Come ye after me, and I will make you to become fishers of men

12. What is their response? (1:18)

They left their nets and followed Him

13. What does Jesus do in the synagogue? (1:21)

He taught,
He also healed a man by casting out an evil spirit

14. What is the reaction of the people? (1:22, 27)

They were astonished and amazed

15. What disturbance takes place in the synagogue? (1:23-26)

Jesus cast an evil spirit from a man

16. What happens next at the house of Simon and Andrew? (1:29-30)

He healed Simon's mother in law

17. What two forms of ministry does Jesus pursue as he goes "throughout Galilee"? (1:39)

preaching in the synagogues and releasing many from the power of demons.

18. What type of person does Mark now mention as coming to Jesus? (1:40)

a leper

19. How does Jesus help this man? (1:41)

He healed him

20. Then what does Jesus charge this man? (1:43-44)

Not to tell anyone and go to the priest and offer the offering prescribed by Moses

21. Instead, what does this man do? (1:45a)

He shouted and told everyone

22. What is the result for Jesus? (1:45b)

He could no longer go into a city but had to be out in desert wastelands

DIMENSION TWO:
WHAT DOES THE BIBLE MEAN?

❏ *Mark 1:1.* The first verse of Mark is essentially the title of the Gospel of Mark. This verse also states the basic conviction the author wants to support with evidence from his account. Thus each word is important.

The word *gospel* means "good news." The name *Jesus* (a revision of *Joshua* meaning "Yahweh saves") was given to the child by his parents at God's direction. (See Luke 1:31.) Linked with Jesus is Christ. The word *Christ* is actually a title, not a last name. The word is used for *Messiah* or *Anointed One* (anointed by God with a special nature and for a special purpose).

Son of God refers to Jesus' divine origin and nature and is a title inherited from the Jewish tradition. Mark writes of Jesus not just as "a" Son of God but as "the" Son of God. We will find these understandings of Jesus coming through the material that Mark remembers and records.

❏ *Mark 1:2-11.* The words quoted by Mark (1:2-3) are actually a combination of Malachi 3:1 and Isaiah 40:3. At the outset, Mark links the figure and events of Jesus' life with the inherited and revered Old Testament tradition. In this way, the new would be seen as an extension and fulfillment of the old. Before a king or ruler would arrive, a herald or messenger would announce his coming in advance so that everyone would be ready. John the Baptist is seen as such a messenger. His call was not for physical preparations, but for spiritual ones. He urged people to enter into an experience of confession of sin. Turning away from sin by God's help ("repentance") would then result in baptism.

John wore garments like those of Elijah. (See 2 Kings 1:8.) Elijah was one of the earliest of the prophets of great influence. John preached in the desert area between Jerusalem and the Jordan River, a distance of thirty miles. It would have been near where the Jordan River empties into the Dead Sea south of the ancient town of Jericho. Judea (Mark 1:5) was a province extending from the Mediterranean Sea on the west to the Jordan River on the east. Judea included the city of Jerusalem.

Through baptism John uses water to symbolize God's washing the people from sin. Moreover, he promises that the One who is coming will not bring a symbolic cleansing but an actual cleansing. This person will be a person from whom the Spirit would enter into their lives.

The dove is a well-known symbol in Jewish spiritual history. Its role is that of a messenger of peace and hope. A dove as a messenger of peace was first seen by Noah when the dove returned to the ark with an olive leaf. The dove let Noah know the destructive waters were receding. (See Genesis 8:8-12.) The voice from heaven (1:11) affirms what Mark has proclaimed in his opening verse (1:1).

❑ *Mark 1:12-13.* Here, on the one hand, is Jesus destitute and in danger from physical and spiritual forces. (Recall Matthew 4:1-11 for details.) On the other hand, we see the supportive protection of providence meeting his need through angels. The battle against Satan and God's protection have begun with Jesus on earth.

❑ *Mark 1:14-22.* Jesus begins his ministry through a proclamation and an invitation. Returning to his home province, Galilee, northeast of Judea, Jesus begins proclaiming to his neighbors that God has now ("the time has come") stepped into their history in a special way. The kingdom of God is at their doorstep. They are to enter through turning away from evil (repenting) and by faith turning to the good news.

The invitation is extended to the fishermen, Simon, Andrew, James, and John, as they carry out their daily tasks. Jesus meets persons and offers them new possibilities, not just for their sakes but for the sake of others. Either because this is what the fishermen deeply want or because of the attractiveness of Jesus, they immediately change their priorities and follow him.

Jesus goes not only to his home province to begin his ministry but also to his home synagogue. There, to those who would recall him simply as a fellow who "grew up here," he amazes them with his keen insight. Instead of being a means through which the authority of God's law (the Torah) is revealed as were the rabbis, Jesus seems to be God's Law himself.

❏ *Mark 1:23-34.* Anyone whose behavior was strange, destructive, and seemingly uncontrollable was thought to be under the control of an unclean spirit. This person, as he disturbs the synagogue session out of his perplexity, is identified by Mark as recognizing Jesus for what he is—the Holy One of God. Amidst physical turmoil, by Jesus' command a release takes place, adding to the people's awe of Jesus. The awe begins to spread.

This cleansing is followed by another expression of care for persons through the healing of Simon's wife's mother. Now throngs with needs seek Jesus out. Mark sees even the evil forces involved in their illnesses as recognizing Jesus. His divine status was obvious even to evil forces.

❏ *Mark 1:35.* Jesus seeks in privacy the spiritual replenishment that will enable him to be God's servant in publicly meeting human need.

❏ *Mark 1:36-45.* Jesus is on the move, from place to place and need to need, as Mark will often describe him.

Leprosy was considered to be an example of disease in its ugliest and most incurable form. By touching a person whom no one would ever touch (verse 41), Jesus imparts healing. Jesus does not call upon persons to break with the Jewish law, but advises the healed man to carry out the obligations of Leviticus 14. Although Jesus calls for special blessings of deliverance to be held in confidence, the man who formerly had suffered from leprosy spreads the word widely. His testimony creates frustration for Jesus who hereafter has to struggle for privacy because of the crowds of curious and needy.

DIMENSION THREE: WHAT DOES THE BIBLE MEAN TO ME?

Jesus as a New Possibility

The study of Mark brings us directly to a unique and valuable account of Jesus' life by an author with eyewitness experiences to recount and some strong convictions to express. As you read Mark, see if you can discover for yourself why this short account is included with the other three Gospels.

At the outset, Mark testifies that Jesus' status as Son of God is confirmed by God's Spirit at his baptism (verses 10-11). This new action by God calls for new reactions by God's people, namely recognizing a new day of God's presence and activity in their midst and offering themselves anew to God for forgiveness and commitment. Do you see God moving in some new ways in our time? What shall our reaction be?

In reading any of the Gospel accounts we usually first look for what is happening in Jesus' life. However, in Mark we need to go further and ask, What does this say about the kind of person Jesus was? Also ask, What does this event suggest about the nature of the other persons in the story? Take these questions and apply them to each of the events in this introductory chapter: the baptism and retreat into the wilderness, the call of the disciples, Jesus' teaching in the synagogue and the people's response, and the healing ministries.

The way Mark begins his narrative immediately testifies to the fact that something of great importance and of a most unusual nature is taking place. With forthrightness, as is Mark's style, he comes to the point in his first sentence! Do you recall it?

Then Mark supports that bold affirmation through all that follows in this chapter. Mark further implies that amazing new possibilities are available for those who will follow Jesus (1:17), or who are "brought to Jesus" (1:32), or who kneel before him (1:40). What new possibilities has Jesus brought into your life? What new possibilities might he bring to you and your class members if you also seriously encounter Jesus in these ways?

In light of Mark's approach, as you begin this study series, you might well ask, Who do I see Jesus really to be? Next you need to ask, What response have I made to his coming? Perhaps you might even try to read Mark again as though you had not come to any convictions about Jesus and see what Mark leads you to believe.

The people heard that he had come home. So many gathered that there was no room left. . . (2:1-2).

— 2 —
The News Went Around
Mark 2–3

DIMENSION ONE:
WHAT DOES THE BIBLE SAY?

Answer these questions by reading Mark 2

1. Where do these events take place? (2:1)

   Capernaum.

2. In what unusual way do persons arrange for the paralyzed man to be brought to Jesus' attention? (2:4)

   They opened roof above Jesus and lowered the sick man down to Jesus, on his stretcher

3. What does Jesus see in the companions of the paralyzed man that brings forth this response? (2:5)

   Their great faith

4. What is Jesus' response to the men's faith? (2:5, 11)

   He healed the sick man

5. What accusation do the critics of Jesus make against him? (2:7) *They accused Him of blasphemy*

6. Of what does Jesus want to convince his critics? (2:10)

That He has the power on earth to forgive sins

7. Where is Levi when Jesus meets him? (2:14)

Sitting at his tax collection booth

8. What invitation does Jesus give to Levi? (2:14)

"Follow me."

9. Who are Jesus' companions at the meal in Levi's house? (2:15)

Other tax collectors and sinners

10. What question do the Pharisees raise? (2:16)

Why did Jesus eat with sinners

11. How does Jesus describe his own calling? (2:17)

That He came not to call the righteous but the sinners to repentance

12. What difference is noted between the disciples of John the Baptist and those of Jesus? (2:18)

They fasted but not Jesus'.

13. What three figures of speech does Jesus use in his reaction? (2:19-22)

Children of the bridegroom or sewing new cloth on a garment or putting new wine in old bottles

14. What new criticism is leveled against Jesus? (2:23-24)

His disciples picked and ate grain as they went and the Pharisees said they were breaking the Sabbath law

15. What Old Testament story does Jesus recall in response? (2:25-26)

How David and his followers ate the bread of the high priest in the Temple when they were hungry.

16. What does Jesus affirm about the sabbath? (2:28)

That the Son of man is Lord also of the sabbath

Answer these questions by reading Mark 3

17. What question does Jesus ask about the sabbath? (3:4)

Is it lawful to do good on the sabbath day, or to do evil? To save life, or to kill?

18. What is the congregation's response? (3:4)

They held their peace. So they might accuse Him when He did heal the man

19. Why does Jesus ask for a boat to be prepared for his use? (3:9)

Because of the many people coming to Him to be healed

20. What direction does Jesus give to the "evil spirits"? (3:12)

He told them that they should not make Him known

21. What are the tasks of the disciples whom Jesus appoints? (3:14-15)

That He would send them forth to preach, heal sicknesses and to cast out devils

22. Who are the persons Jesus appoints? (3:16-19)

1. Simon Peter
2. James (son of Zebedee) and his brother John Boanerges (sons of thunder) 3.
4. Andrew 5. Philip, 6. Bartholomew, 7. Matthew, 8 Thomas 9 James (son of Alphaeus)
10. Thaddaeus, 11. Simon (the Canaanite), 12 Judas Iscariot (betrayer)

23. How do the critics of Jesus explain his actions? (3:22)

That he had Beelzebub the prince of devils

24. With what figures of speech does Jesus respond? (3:24-27)

25. What sin does Jesus indicate cannot be forgiven? (3:29)

Blaspheme against the Holy Ghost

DIMENSION TWO:
WHAT DOES THE BIBLE MEAN?

Two contrasting attitudes appear in Mark's account of the ministry of Jesus. One is that of popular appeal and the other is that of constant criticism. Note that the two attitudes are often present at the same time and place. Each positive action that increases Jesus' admirers also stimulates and may enlarge his negative critics.

❏ *Mark 2:1-2.* Jesus returns from his private spiritual retreat and the visit to surrounding towns to the central city of the area, Capernaum. Now what Simon had told Jesus earlier (1:37) proves to be true: people in increasingly large numbers gather wherever Jesus goes, including those with various needs.

❏ *Mark 2:3-4.* Palestinian houses had flat roofs that often served the function of being what a porch or patio is to us.

They had a stairway leading up to it from the side of the house. Up the four men went with their paralyzed companion to the flat rooftop. Then through an enlarged skylight opening or a newly created opening they lowered the litter to a spot in front of Jesus.

❑ *Mark 2:5-12.* So many persons are attracted to Jesus that these men cannot get their paralyzed friend in through the door. A group of persons who are highly critical of what Jesus does is also in the crowd. In ministering to the sick man, Jesus recognizes the close interrelation of spirit, mind, and body. In illness the total person must receive therapy for complete healing to take place. In this instance Jesus perceives a sense of guilt within the paralyzed man that is a part of his illness. Jesus offers him forgiveness.

Specialists in Jewish law, sometimes called scribes, knew that Isaiah 43:25 stated that God alone could forgive sin and accuse Jesus of blasphemy. Blasphemy is the offense of presuming to act or speak in the place of or with no respect for God. Blasphemy occurs when a person presumes to be God or to act like there is no God. The penalty for blasphemy is death by stoning (see Leviticus 24:16). Already, early in Jesus' ministry, the possibility of creating legal grounds for his death is taking place.

The story ends with a tremendous tribute (verse 12) in the midst of strong criticism.

❑ *Mark 2:13-17.* Capernaum (2:1) was on the shore of the Sea of Galilee. Levi is thought to have been the same person as Matthew (see Matthew 10:3). Jesus comes to Levi in the midst of his daily work as a tax collector. This episode introduces what follows—a meal with several other "tax collectors and 'sinners' " (2:15). Again Jesus is criticized, but he sees himself as a physician who seeks out persons in need of his help.

❑ *Mark 2:18-22.* In this passage the relationship of the old with the new is opened for discussion. John the Baptist was an ascetic, rejecting social customs and common attire. Jesus enters into many customs but with a purging influence. Jesus leads people away from the old legalistic religion and its practices, exposing them to new spiritual expressions.

❏ *Mark 2:23-28.* These two events deal with a common theme: a new understanding of the sabbath. While accused of violating the sabbath by picking grain, Jesus points his critics to 1 Samuel 21:1-6 where David took sacred bread from the altar to feed his hungry soldiers. In the midst of a healing act on the sabbath, Jesus raises the question as to what, after all, is the purpose of the sabbath. The sabbath was intended to meet human need, and to meet such needs is a fulfillment of the sabbath.

❏ *Mark 3:1-6.* The beginning of Jesus' ministry and miracles are rejected by the stubbornness of the Pharisees.

❏ *Mark 3:7-19.* Again the crowds come, and Jesus must use a boat from which to teach in order to avoid harm from the crowd's size. Sensing he alone cannot meet their immense needs, Jesus appoints twelve to be his co-ministers. *Apostles* means "those who are sent out." Mark includes the calling of the Twelve to emphasize "that they might be with him and that he might send them out," against the background of which people hail Jesus and reject Jesus.

❏ *Mark 3:20-27.* Even Jesus' family begins to question his sanity or his propriety. Since all strange or uncommon human behavior in that day was seen to be the result of spirits or demons, the scribes attributed Jesus' actions to the power of Beelzebub, a word traceable to the idolatrous Baal worshiped in Old Testament days and seen as a powerful demon in Jesus' day. Note that now the scribes have moved from the accusation of "blasphemy" to Jesus being the servant of the Devil. Jesus responds in part by implying that the good he has been doing would not be done by an evil one.

❏ *Mark 3:28-30.* No verse has been the source of more perplexity leading to misuse and even fear than verse 29. What is it that the Holy Spirit does? The Spirit in various ways points us toward our need for God and God's gracious forgiveness. If we never respond to the Spirit's prodding and never seek God or God's forgiveness, it is not so much that God will not forgive us as it is that we have never sought or found that which is readily available from God.

❏ *Mark 3:31-35.* Compare verses 21 and 32; they may be interrelated. It could be that Jesus now realized that those outside his own family may understand him better than his own kin. In any event, Jesus opens the door to a multitude to be a part of the intimacy of his family—if they have the same priority (verse 35).

DIMENSION THREE:
WHAT DOES THE BIBLE MEAN TO ME?

Invitation to New Possibilities

In the scope of these two chapters many insights and issues arise that merit a lot of pondering. In increasing numbers persons are coming to Jesus. Look over the two chapters and identify some of the different types of persons (such as the physically ill, emotionally disturbed, religious leaders, corrupt government officials, family members, and so forth). What was there about Jesus that attracted so many different types of persons?

The purpose and use of the sabbath is brought forward as an issue. Jesus points us away from legalisms in determining what is right or wrong for the sabbath. He points us toward the basic question as to what was, and is, the intent of the sabbath. In that light what should determine our use of the sabbath? This new standard for the sabbath is what enhances and preserves personhood and the basic needs of persons as God's creations, loved by God. Therefore, what do you think it would mean for you and your group for "the Son of Man" to be "Lord even of the Sabbath" (2:28)?

The so-called "unforgivable sin" is identified (3:29). What have you thought that meant? Remember that the context for this is a rebuke by Jesus against the spiritual narrowness and judgmental attitudes of the religious leadership. Jesus has to break through spiritual prejudices to convey what God's Spirit wants him to say. Not only spiritual indifference can keep us from responding to God's Spirit. Spiritual arrogance and close-mindedness can also blind and block us to the new truths God's Spirit would teach us. This attitude is pathetic as well as one that can become potentially unforgivable.

The beautiful invitation remains, however. Any of us who are open to new possibilities (2:9-10), new discipleship (2:14), new redemptive relationships (2:15-16), new lifestyles (2:19), new usages of sacred bequests (2:27-28), new responsibilities while we are with Jesus (3:14-15), and a new openness to the Spirit's leadership are welcome to the intimacy and hope of Jesus' family circle (3:35).

He taught them many things by parables (4:2).

3
The Master Teacher
Mark 4:1-34

DIMENSION ONE:
WHAT DOES THE BIBLE SAY?

Answer these questions by reading Mark 4:1-34

1. Where does Jesus begin to teach? (4:1)

   He spoke from a ship on the sea and the people on shore

2. Where does Jesus carry this out? (4:1)

   From the boat

3. How does Jesus communicate with his hearers? (4:2)

   By parables

4. Who is the subject of the first story Jesus tells? (4:3)

   The one who sows the seed

5. Where do the seeds fall as they are thrown from the sower's hand? (4:4-8)

Some fell by wayside
some on stony ground
some among thorns
some on good ground

6. What happened to the seeds in the various places where they fell? (4:4-8)

Seed was eaten by fowl
Some on stony ground, grew up but was scorched by sun
and others the thorns choked it
but that on good soil, grew and yielded much fruit.

7. To whom, does Jesus say, has the secret of the kingdom of God been given? (4:11)

To the followers

8. How do those outside the kingdom of God react to the parables? (4:12)

They didn't understand

9. In the interpretation by Jesus, what is the sower represented as sowing? (4:14)

The word of God

10. What regrettable things happen in some persons who receive what the sower distributes? (4:15-19)

They hear the Word but Satan steals it away, others receive it gladly but only endure for a time, others are choked off by the cares of the world

11. What hopeful things happen in those persons who are the "good soil"? (4:20)

That they receive the Word and bring forth much fruit.

12. What is the next figure of speech Jesus uses? (4:21)

About a candle

13. What is supposed to be done with it? (4:21-22)

It is to be put on a candlestick and not put under a bushel or under a bed

14. What lesson does Jesus draw from this parable? (4:22)

That nothing was hid or secret but would be broadcast

15. What determines what we receive? (4:24)

Jesus' Word

16. What contrast does Jesus draw between one who has and one who has not? (4:25)

The one who has, more will be given (faith) Those who has little or none, shall lose even that.

17. What happens to the seed sown in the next parable? (4:26-29)

The seed grows and produces but the planter doesn't know how

18. What figure of speech does Jesus next use to describe the kingdom of God? (4:31)

It is like a mustard seed.

19. What is unusual about this kind of seed? (4:31)

It is very small

20. How often did Jesus use parables in his public teaching? (4:33-34) *Many times*

21. What did he do privately with his disciples? (4:34)

He explained what the parables meant.

DIMENSION TWO:
WHAT DOES THE BIBLE MEAN?

Up to this point in Mark, most of the teachings of Jesus that we have encountered have been statements in response to events that have taken place. Often Jesus' teachings have been explanations given in reaction to criticisms. Now we encounter teachings of Jesus that do not appear to be tied to a specific event. Of course, they are related to the whole nature of his ministry and what is happening as a result of it.

❏ *Mark 4:1-2.* Here Jesus is teaching outdoors and away from an urban setting. Outdoors was the more usual setting for Jesus' teaching. At the beginning of his ministry, Jesus apparently sought to use the synagogue as the place for his teaching (Matthew 13:53-54; Luke 4:16-21). However, negative reaction from Jewish religious leaders soon forced this practice to cease. So Jesus moved to the open air for his teaching.

These introductory verses also tell us that Jesus often taught through the use of parables. You may already be familiar with the well-known definition of a parable as being "an earthly story with a heavenly meaning." A parable is a story that conveys insight through using well-known or observable happenings as similar to what also happens on a deeper level of life. In using parables to teach, Jesus was following a form of teaching used often by Jewish religious teachers and by the Old Testament prophets. Can you recall some of these? Among the better known parables that you might like to read again are Joseph's dreams (Genesis 37:5; 41:15-36), Nathan's story of the pet lamb (2 Samuel 12:1-6), Isaiah's song of the vineyard (5:1-10), and the whole story of Jonah (1–4).

Mark 4 is made up of a series of parables. However, these are not the first parables Jesus has used in Mark. For instance, in the last lesson we saw brief parables in Jesus' references to the unshrunk cloth (2:21), new wine (2:22), and the burglary in the strong man's house (3:27).

❑ *Mark 4:3-9.* Part of Jesus' genius as a teacher is the way in which he could identify and use in his teaching figures of speech and events that would be easily understood by his hearers. He used examples that were a part of his hearers' daily lives. These examples would capture the people's attention and easily bring insight to them in an understandable form. All of Jesus' hearers had seen sowers and many of them were sowers. In that arid, rocky country they knew about shallow soil, rocky ground, and wild thorns. They knew that a key to success in growing crops was finding the right soil.

❑ *Mark 4:10-12.* In this puzzling statement to the disciples, Jesus points out what is often true. To those who enter seriously into discipleship, spiritual discoveries leap out everywhere. For those who are outside the frame of reference that discipleship brings, truth passes close by, unnoticed and undiscovered. Can you recall in your life the difference serious discipleship has made in your ability to make discoveries?

❑ *Mark 4:13-20.* Here Jesus interprets the parable of the sower for his disciples. In some cases he leaves it to his hearers to make the interpretation, but not in this case. Four types of response to the word that God spreads are described. Each should be noted carefully. Can you think of illustrations from today of each of these types of response?

In speaking of those described in verses 16-17 who "receive [the word] with joy" but who do not allow it to root, *The Revised English Bible* has a striking translation: "They have no staying-power." Is that so with you?

❑ *Mark 4:21-23.* The word *bowl* seems to have an unusual usage at this point. What the text is referring to is a container, like a pot, that would hold a bushel of produce. Sometimes such a container turned upside down might be used as a lampstand. A lantern is placed on it, not under it. The lantern is placed where it can achieve its purpose, its reason for being, which is to provide light. If this happens, everything (all truth) is seen.

❑ *Mark 4:24-25.* Jesus uses another familiar figure of speech in these verses, familiar to women and men alike—a measure. This proposal is the opposite of what we expect. "As we give, so we receive; as we keep, so we lose." (Read Luke's rendering of this statement, 6:37-38.) What relevance does this example have for your own sharing of what you have?

❑ *Mark 4:26-29.* Here Jesus returns to the image of the sower. This time the emphasis is not on what the sower does but on what happens after the sower's job is done. Beyond the sower's power to bring it about, the corn grows on its own. God is able to bring forth God's things from the small thing the sower does. We should do all we can and faithfully carry out our responsibilities. Then we must let go and let God do immeasurably more than all we can ask or conceive by, "the power which is at work among us" (Ephesians 3:20, *The Revised English Bible*).

❑ *Mark 4:30-32.* The mustard plant begins from a very small seed. Some people think Jesus is referring to a plant in Galilee by a similar name that grows to over six feet in height. Others think Jesus was intentionally describing abnormal growth to make a point by exaggeration. Either way, the growth illustrates the power of little when God is part of the process. Clarence Jordan translates verse 32 unforgettably by describing the seed as "lifting a clod of dirt twenty times bigger than it was, just pushin', sayin', 'Get out of the way, clod, I'm movin' to God' " (*Cotton Patch Parables of Liberation,* Herald Press, 1976; page 125).

❑ *Mark 4:33-34.* On every occasion Jesus tried to teach with illustrations from the ordinary and the commonplace. The meanings were usually obvious, but in their private conversations later, Jesus could explain to his disciples meanings that were overlooked or obscure (as he did in verses 10-20).

DIMENSION THREE:
WHAT DOES THE BIBLE MEAN TO ME?

What Is the Purpose of Parables?

Jesus' use of parables, as illustrated in Mark, is both a beautiful and a skillful form of teaching. It is beautiful in that excellent word-pictures are created for the hearer. Truth becomes visualized in memorable ways. Helmut Thielicke, a noted German pastor, has described the parables of Jesus as "God's picturebook" (*The Waiting Father,* Harper and Row, 1959; page 11).

In the sample of parables provided in Mark 4, we see how Jesus uses parables for different purposes. The first way parables are used is to inform our minds and enlarge our understanding (the secret growth described in 4:26-29). The second way parables are used is to influence our attitudes or feelings about persons or issues (the call for large expectations suggested by the story of the mustard seed in 4:30-32). The third way parables are used is to prod our actions, to encourage us to do something (to give and not just to receive as appears in 4:24-25). Re-examine the parables in Mark 4 in this light and see what you feel is their intent. Also keep this in mind as you read other parables used by Jesus.

The gospel itself has all three purposes: to inform our minds, to influence our attitudes, and to prod our actions. Unless it moves in all three ways into our experience, we have only discovered the gospel in part.

Jesus' particular use of this method demonstrates his insightful skill in communicating with his audience. The figures of speech and the subjects of his parables are borrowed from the everyday activities and observations of his hearers (sowers and seed, lamps in rooms where windows were not common, trading practices, growth processes). As Jesus spoke in this fashion, he not only used illustrations his hearers could easily understand but also by doing so he conveyed the sense that he knew and understood their lifestyles. He not only transmitted truth, but a sense of identification or empathy with his hearers as well. He even raised one's daily experiences to be seen as the laboratory for discoveries of God's ways and purposes.

What about our own experience and expressions of our faith? Can we see God in the commonplace? Is it possible for us not only to want to tell the world about God but also to find God in our daily lives? The tradition Jesus inherited was one in which God was experienced in events that touched their lives. Not in rare mystical moments but in daily experiences God was revealed to patriarchs, kings, seekers, and prophets. We can see God revealed to us if we have eyes to see and ears to hear God in the commonplace.

Who is this? Even the wind and the waves
obey him (4:41b)!

— 4 —
The Miracle Worker
Mark 4:35–6:6

DIMENSION ONE:
WHAT DOES THE BIBLE SAY?

Answer these questions by reading Mark 4:35-41

1. Where is Jesus heading and with whom? (4:35-36)

   Across the Sea of Galilee with his disciples

2. What unexpected misfortune do they encounter? (4:37)

   A bad storm.

3. Where is Jesus at this time? (4:38)

   He was asleep

4. What do the disciples cry out to Jesus? (4:38)

   "Master, careth thou not that we perish?"

5. What does Jesus do? (4:39-40)

He calmed the wind and the sea

6. What is the reaction of the disciples? (4:41)

They were afraid.
Because Jesus could control the wind
and the sea

Answer these questions by reading Mark 5

7. What is the shocking nature of the person Jesus meets on
   arriving at the other side of the lake? (5:2-5) What is this
   person's name? (5:9)

He was full of demons,
He said his name was Legion

8. What does this person shout out to Jesus? (5:7)

"What have I to do with thee, Jesus, thou Son of the most
high God? I adjure thee by God, that thou torment me not."

9. What does Jesus say to the tormented one? (5:8) What
   strange result takes place? (5:11-13)

"Come out of the man, thou unclean spirit"
The evil spirits leave the man and enter into
a large herd of pigs

10. When the people come to see what was happening, what
    do they see? (5:14-15) What are their reactions? (5:15, 17)

They saw their pigs drowned in the sea and the
man in his right mind.
They were afraid and wanted Jesus to leave

11. What is the healed man's request? (5:18)

He wanted to go with Jesus.

12. Instead, what different direction does Jesus give him? (5:19) What does the man do? (5:20)

Jesus told him to go home and tell his friends what great things the Lord did for him. So he went to Decapolis and told everyone.

13. Who is Jairus, and what request does he make? (5:22-23)

He was the leader of the local synagogue. He wanted Jesus to heal his little daughter who was near death.

14. How does Jesus respond? (5:24a)

He went with him.

15. What is the need of the next person among the crowd who seeks out Jesus? (5:25-26) Why does she turn to him? (5:27-28)

A woman who had been sick for 12 years, and getting worse. She had heard of Jesus' healing miracles.

16. What does she do, and what is the result? (5:27-29)

She touched his robe, and was healed.

17. What question does Jesus ask? (5:30)

"Who touched me?"

18. What is the woman's feeling in response to his question? (5:33)

She is very fearful but told the truth — that she was healed

19. What reassurance does Jesus give her? (5:34)

" Daughter, thy faith hath made thee whole; go in peace, and be whole of thy plague

20. What sad news comes from the ruler's house? (5:35)

They told Jairus his daughter was dead

21. What counsel does Jesus give? (5:36)

" Be not afraid, only believe "

22. What is Jesus' reaction to the grief at the house of Jairus? (5:39)

" Why make ye this ado, and weep? the damsel is not dead, but sleepeth."

23. What amazing event then takes place? (5:40-43)

He took her by the hand and told her to get up and she arose and walked about. He told them not to tell any one and she should have something to eat.

Answer these questions by reading Mark 6:1-6

24. Where do Jesus and the disciples go? (6:1)

They left there and came into his own country

25. What is the synagogue congregation's reaction to Jesus? (6:2-3) *When He preached at the synagogue, they wondered about His wisdom and mighty works because He was a carpenter with 4 brothers and sisters*

26. In this connection what does Jesus say about a prophet? (6:4) *A prophet is not without honor, but in his own country, and among his own kin, and in his own house.*

27. What was the effect of their reaction on Jesus' ministry there? (6:5-6) *He could do no mighty works but healed a few sick. He went about, teaching.*

DIMENSION TWO:
WHAT DOES THE BIBLE MEAN?

"Who is this?" Mark has no doubt as to the answer. He told us his conviction in 1:1—"the gospel about Jesus Christ, the Son of God." This portion of Mark is a dramatic support for this conviction.

❑ *Mark 4:35-41.* With the disciples Jesus sails across the Sea of Galilee. This beautiful body of water is surrounded by high hills, some fairly steep. It is like a cup with the sea at the bottom of the cup. When storm winds blow across that area, they come down the sides of the hills with increasing force and churn up the tranquil lake suddenly with high waves and strong currents. Once I experienced this weather as I crossed the Sea of Galilee in a launch. A storm came up with such strong winds and waves that one of the two motors of our boat became disabled. We had to change course for a different destination.

Having spent the day teaching and reacting to the crowd, Jesus falls asleep while sailing. Out of fear the disciples wake him shouting, "Don't you care?" (4:38). Jesus speaks a command that calms the sea and also speaks a word to calm the disciples' anxious spirits (4:40). Jesus was apparently as much concerned over the anxiety of the disciples in their stormy reaction to the unexpected as he was about the storm waves around them. The disciples are awed by his mastery of both.

❏ *Mark 5:1-9.* At first reading this story may seem bizarre. Remember, however, that in spite of modern translations we are still looking at ancient events through primitive perspectives. Here a man is encountered who is mentally ill, as characterized by abnormal behavior beyond his control. Because he could not exercise self-control, he was seen to be under someone else's control—an evil spirit or demon. Like too many victims of mental illness in our day, he was misunderstood and rejected. The only "treatment" was "chains and irons" and isolation from society (like institutions far away from home). As a result, his condition worsened with his inability to sleep and deep depression until he became suicidal.

Since this man had received society's torment, which was as bad as the torment of his own illness, seeing Jesus coming he expected the same treatment from him. Jesus deals with the man on his level of understanding ("Come out . . . , you evil spirit!" 5:8). The sick man called himself "Legion," a military term referring to a regiment of about six thousand men. Angels or demons were understood as being organized in such groups. Legion was his way of referring to his condition of possessing many personalities.

❏ *Mark 5:10-20.* This section deals with results of the deliverance brought by Jesus. To the primitive viewpoint, when demons left a person, they had to go somewhere. This multitude of demons ("Legion") had to go somewhere; so they are portrayed as going into a herd of pigs. This herd stampedes and falls over a hillside into the nearby Sea of Galilee.

Word spread to the nearby area; and persons came, curious to see what had happened. Whereas once they were afraid of the behavior of the ill man, now they are afraid of him because he is well. (Is this fear typical of our attitudes toward those who have received treatment for mental illness?) The people preferred for Jesus to leave ("the people began to plead with Jesus to leave their region").

The man's reaction is to want to cling to Jesus, his understanding therapist. But Jesus wants him to help others. God's gracious gifts are not for our private enjoyment but for contagious sharing. To his home and the ten nearby cities (called in Greek "the Decapolis") he went witnessing to what God in mercy had done through Jesus (5:19-20).

❑ *Mark 5:21-24, 35-43.* These two sections tell the story of the healing of Jairus's daughter. Jairus was a synagogue ruler. Because of the increasing opposition of religious leaders to Jesus, it is remarkable that Jairus would come. However, prejudices are often dropped when desperate needs occur. The story is filled with drama, because word comes en route that Jairus's daughter has died. Yet Jesus still encourages him to have faith (for new possibilities, a theme of Mark). Indeed, this faith is rewarded. As Jesus speaks the word (5:41), the child responds. Again the people are in awe of Jesus, a characteristic of Mark's accounts. In contrast to the instructions given to the demon-possessed man, Jesus tells these witnesses not to tell others what had taken place.

❑ *Mark 5:25-34.* The interrupting event is that of a woman with chronic internal bleeding. Her prolonged problem deepened her sense of desperate need and her hope that to touch Jesus' garment would bring healing. Jesus sensed that a need had been met and reaffirms faith as the key to new possibilities.

❑ *Mark 6:1-6.* This collection by Mark of miraculous ministries by Jesus ends with Jesus returning to his hometown (Nazareth), not far from the Sea of Galilee. His reputation as teacher and miracle worker had preceded him. This congregation of homefolks had trouble putting together the record of Jesus' achievements with their image of the hometown boy. Mark suggests that Jesus' teaching on the parables and his healing ministries are not well accepted. The sentence Jesus quotes about a prophet is not from the Bible but may have been a common proverb. As for the people, fixed attitudes from the past prevent new possibilities for the future from Jesus to them (6:6).

DIMENSION THREE:
WHAT DOES THE BIBLE MEAN TO ME?

The Miracles

Although we have encountered miracles earlier in Mark, these verses contain the largest collection of miracles in any one section of Mark. This unusual collection is obviously here for a purpose. Do you recall the verse in Mark where the writer states his theme? It is the presentation of the good news of Jesus Christ as "Son of God." John the Baptist describes Jesus as "more powerful than I" (1:7). Early in his account Mark wants the reader to identify Jesus as this mighty one, even the Son of God. Jesus' miraculous ministries are recorded to convince the reader of the truth of this conviction.

As you look at the entire section, you realize that the stories tell us of the total mastery of Jesus: over the physical elements (4:41), the demoniac (5:8), animal life (5:13), physical illness (5:28-29), and even death itself (5:41-42). Mark wants us to know that these miracles are divinity in action—the Son of God has come. Even the tormented one identifies Jesus as "Son of the Most High God" (5:7). The awe felt by those observing (4:41; 5:15, 20, 27, 42; 6:2) reinforces this awareness of the divine presence in Jesus.

Of course, these records of the miraculous leave any serious Bible student with many of the same kinds of questions as were expressed by Jesus' own home congregation (6:2-3). For Mark the explanation of the miraculous is simple yet profound—Jesus was the Son of God. Some of us may want more explanation but it is really not to be found. We must understand and enter into the faith perspective of the writer, knowing that all marvelous experiences of deliverance and healing in any form are miracles of grace, and experience is always more than can be reported by pen.

Furthermore, as Mark implies, Jesus brings into the midst of life's unexpected bruises, prolonged hurts, and desperate hours his own presence, concern, understanding, and help. Only our lack of receptivity precludes this. The crowds were all around, many with similar needs, but those with a hopeful and receptive spirit discovered and received God's gracious deliverances.

From this awareness comes the discovery of God's new possibilities for us and for those who hurt and whose hurts have been overlooked or unheeded by the crowds. We who have received God's gracious deliverance are called to a special sensitivity to such persons. Who are they around you?

Calling the Twelve to him, he sent them out
two by two . . . (6:7a).

—— **5** ——

Under Orders

Mark 6:7-56

DIMENSION ONE:
WHAT DOES THE BIBLE SAY?

Answer these questions by reading Mark 6:7-56

1. Whom does Jesus call? (6:7)

   (The twelve)

2. Why does Jesus call them? (6:7)

   To send them forth, two by two

3. What authority does Jesus give them? (6:7)

   He gave them power over unclean spirits

4. What are they to take? What are they to leave behind? (6:8-9) Take nothing for their journey except a staff

   No scrip, no bread, no money.

   Wear sandals and wear one coat

5. When are they to stay at a place? When are they to leave? (6:10-11) *To stay at a house til time to leave the place.*

6. What did they do and achieve on their first mission? (6:12-13) *They preached that men should repent and cast out many devils and healed the sick*

7. How does Herod hear of Jesus? (6:14a)
He thought That John the Baptist had risen from the dead

8. What are the rumors about Jesus? (6:14b-15)
Others said He was Elias (Elijah) others said He was a prophet.

9. What is Herod's opinion of John? (6:16)
He thought that Jesus was John, who he beheaded had risen from the dead

10. What had Herod done to John the Baptist? Why? (6:17-18)
Beheaded him

11. What role do Herodias and her daughter play in this tragedy? (6:19-25)

12. What is Herod's opinion of John the Baptist? (6:20) What was his personal feeling about Herodias's daughter's request? (6:26)

13. What does Herod do about the request? (6:27) Why? (6:26)

14. What happens to the body of John the Baptist? (6:28-29)

15. What invitation does Jesus convey to his disciples when they return from their mission? (6:30-31)

16. What happens when they try to do this? (6:32-33)

17. What is Jesus' feeling about these people? (6:34)

18. What problem develops related to the crowd? (6:35-36)

19. What suggestions does Jesus make? (6:37-38)

20. What process does Jesus use to meet the need? (6:39-41)

21. What are the results? (6:42-44, 52)

22. Where does Jesus go? (6:45-46)

23. When and where does Jesus next meet the disciples? (6:47-49)

24. What happens then? (6:50-52)

25. Who are brought to Jesus, and what do they do? (6:53-56)

DIMENSION TWO:
WHAT DOES THE BIBLE MEAN?

Up until now Jesus' ministry as reported by Mark has been essentially a solo ministry. Jesus has been carrying out his mission while others have been observers and "learners" (which is what *disciple* means). Now Jesus expands his ministry by involving others in his mission. The portion of Mark studied in this lesson introduces us to the *nature, price,* and *possibilities* of mission. Look for these elements as you study Mark 6:7-56.

❑ *Mark 6:7-13.* Jesus is teaching the disciples ("the Twelve"). Mark gives a prominent place to the teaching role of Jesus. Notice also that just prior to the beginning of this renewed teaching effort, Mark reports that Jesus "was amazed at their lack of faith." Do you think this statement and Jesus' renewed teaching effort could be related? In what way?

In 1:16-20 Jesus called four of the twelve disciples. In 3:13-19 Jesus appointed twelve to preach and cast out demons. In 6:7-13 Jesus follows through on his intent to "send them out." We noted earlier that the word *apostle* literally means one who is "sent out." In giving them "authority over evil spirits" (the destructive forces within persons that rob them of God's intent for them as expressed in 3:15), the Twelve move out in mission in Jesus' name and spirit.

Note that simplicity of their possessions and wardrobe that Jesus directs is to be a part of their lifestyle while on mission. The "staff" would be like a walking stick or perhaps a shepherd's staff. By taking no bread, bag, or money, the disciples were in effect being called on for absolute dependence on God's providence. This dependence summoned them to be persons of strong faith. God is always more important than everything else.

❑ *Mark 6:14-29.* The Jews awaited a messiah who might be a royal personage. Because of the greatness of the person there would be a messenger or herald to prepare the way by announcing his coming. Since a prophet was God's spokesperson, it was commonly thought that Elijah, one of the earliest and greatest of the prophets, would come in advance of the Messiah to be the messenger. (See Malachi 4:5.) John the Baptist served in this role for Jesus.

In this passage we meet Herod for the first time in Mark's narrative. Many of us tend to think only one Herod ruled in Palestine, but actually a line of Herods served the Romans as rulers. The Herod family were Jewish in origin but only slightly interested in Jewish religious activities. Beginning with Herod the Great, who was ruling as king when Jesus was born, they were appointed by the Romans to various governmental posts in Jewish areas. They were primarily concerned with preventing rebellion.

Herod Antipas, son of Herod the Great, was ruling as Tetrarch (regional governor) of Galilee and Perea when John the Baptist was alive. Herod had divorced his wife to marry Herodias, who was the wife of his half-brother Herod Philip and daughter of another half-brother, Aristobulus. The daughter of Herodias and Herod Philip was named Salome.

Herod Antipas apparently had mixed feelings about John the Baptist—respecting him while bothered by him. These feelings are mirrored in Herod's suspicion that Jesus was John the Baptist raised from the dead. Toward Jesus, Herod probably had the same mixed feelings, as well as a haunting sense of guilt over what he had done to John the Baptist.

Swayed by emotion, Herod made a promise. A public figure's reputation rested on whether his or her promises were carried out. Herodias, who despised John for his denunciation of their marriage, could not overcome Herod's awe of John to get action against him. However, using her daughter's charm, she managed to get an unsuspecting Herod into a position where he would have to provide what she wanted. Because of the public nature of his promise to her daughter, Herod would have to keep the promise.

This story raises several ethical questions: What takes precedence—a promise or the results of a promise? How can we be open to the ideas of others but also true to our sense of right and wrong? How do we avoid making commitments that in time will haunt us?

We can only imagine the hurt of John's disciples as they lovingly bury the body of their leader.

❑ *Mark 6:30-31*. Here is revealed Jesus' sensitivity to the needs of his co-workers. Knowing their weariness as they return from missional activity and perhaps their inner turmoil and grief over word about the death of John, Jesus invites them to go apart with him to rest. Jesus demonstrated this pattern of involvement and withdrawal and knew its value and necessity.

❏ *Mark 6:32-44.* Again their privacy is interrupted, a frequent occurrence in Mark's account. Verse 34 identifies for us the "shepherd's heart" on the part of Jesus. As the hours pass and the people linger, the disciples become concerned about food for everyone. Jesus first bids the disciples to use their own resources, then find what other resources are available and use them. The disciples are frustrated in their attempts to provide food for the crowd. So Jesus takes the loaves and fish. Then an amazing feeding process takes place. What could Jesus do with the little we have to offer if we were willing to offer it?

The event of feeding the multitude is recorded in all four Gospels (Matthew 14:13-21; Luke 9:10-17; John 6:1-13). Perhaps this suggests that the Gospel writers used a common source, perhaps an account independent of the Gospels, to obtain this information. This story probably was part of the oral tradition passed on from person to person by the large crowd which was there. It certainly indicates the importance that each writer attached to this event.

The "twelve basketfuls" probably refers to the fact that twelve disciples were gathering the baskets, although some see this as symbolic of the twelve tribes of Israel.

❏ *Mark 6:45-52.* Note again the withdrawal of Jesus to pray. Note also the contrast between the peaceful isolation of Jesus and the stormy struggle of the disciples. The "fourth watch" was between 3 A.M. and 6 A.M. in the darkest part of the night. In the darkest hour Jesus comes to them, responding to their need in such haste that he almost misses them in passing. Jesus not only speaks comforting words of hope and assurance, he gets into their boat with the disciples. Then the stormy wind ceases. You might like to compare this story with the earlier episode on the sea (4:35-41) discussed in Lesson 4.

One of the ideas advanced by Mark is that a gradual hardening of the heart happened to many toward Jesus as his ministry continued.

❏ *Mark 6:53-56.* Gennesaret may have been the seaside farming area next to Capernaum. So Jesus is returning to his base of ministry. In Mark we notice a pattern of segments of narrative concluding with the crowds pressing around Jesus to receive his ministry to their needs. Here again the crowds rush to him, this time with an added element from the healing episode in 5:25-34. Originally, the sick wanted Jesus to touch them to bring healing. Now they feel if they can only touch Jesus healing will come.

DIMENSION THREE:
WHAT DOES THE BIBLE MEAN TO ME?

Focusing on Mission

The episodes in this section of Mark focus on mission. In various ways they help us sense the nature, price, and possibilities of mission. Mission involves sacrifice and could even involve death (for example, John the Baptist). That we do mission is more important than what we have to do mission with. Christ will take what we have to offer and multiply our offering beyond expectation. A sensitivity to human need around us is a mark of a person in mission and a responsiveness to that need. We should beware that our hearts do not become hardened to new discoveries of God's activities around us. In the process Christ enters into our need as we seek to enter into the needs of others.

Everyone can be Christ's missioners if we open ourselves to be sensitive to others' needs and are willing to pay the price. In what ways do you see yourself in mission? In what ways can you become Christ's servant in mission? To what extent are we responsible for feeding the hungry? Do we need to change our lifestyle in order to feed the hungry?

And he said to them: "You have a fine way of setting aside the commands of God in order to observe your traditions!" (7:9).

—— 6 ——
Old Ways in a New Day
Mark 7

DIMENSION ONE:
WHAT DOES THE BIBLE SAY?

Answer these questions by reading Mark 7

1. Who are meeting with Jesus as this chapter begins? (7:1)

   Pharisees and scribes

2. What do they observe? (7:2)

   They saw that the disciples ate bread without first washing their hands

3. What customs does eating with unwashed hands violate? (7:3-4)

   To cleanse oneself from 'evil' before receiving food.

4. What question do the Pharisees and teachers of the law ask? (7:5)

Why didn't His disciples wash their hands before eating?

5. What does Jesus call these critics? (7:6)

Hypocrites

6. What Old Testament quotation does Jesus use in his response to these questioners? (7:6-7)

7. What three accusations does Jesus make against them? (7:8-9, 13)

8. What illustration does Jesus give of their misuse of tradition? (7:10-12)

9. What parable does Jesus tell his hearers? (7:14-15)

10. How does Jesus explain this parable? (7:18-23)

11. What samples does Jesus name of the evils that can come from inside? (7:21-22)

12. Where does Jesus go? (7:24)

Into the border of Tyre and Sidon and entered into a house

13. What observation does Mark make about Jesus and the public? (7:24)

That He could not be hid

14. Who falls down at the feet of Jesus? (7:25-26)

A Greek woman

15. What is her request? (7:25-26)

That the devil be cast out of her young daughter

16. What exchange of ideas takes place between Jesus and the woman? (7:27-29)

17. What does she find when she returns home? (7:30)

The devil gone and her daughter healed

18. To what area does Jesus now move? (7:31)

Decapolis on coast of Galilee

19. What physical conditions does the person have who is brought to Jesus? (7:32)

deaf and speech impediment

20. What method does Jesus use to meet this man's need? (7:33-34)

He healed him

21. What does *Ephphatha* mean? (7:34)

' Be opened '

22. What happens to the man? (7:35)

His ears were opened and he spoke plain

23. What instructions does Jesus give to those present at this event? What do they do in response? (7:36)

Jo tell no one

24. What is the reaction of those who hear their report? (7:37)

The more they told.

They were amazed.

DIMENSION TWO:
WHAT DOES THE BIBLE MEAN?

As Jesus moves more widely and deeply into his ministry, two important questions begin to occur in the minds of some of his observers: (1) Is Jesus seeking to replace the old religious tradition with something new? (2) What is the relation and relevance of Jesus to the non-Jewish and Gentile world? In the past the Jews had held to their religious tradition as something precious and unique to Jews only. Is the intention of Jesus' ministry to create a new community under a new law? Chapter 7 focuses on this issue.

❏ *Mark 7:1-5.* Refer to Mark 2:23–3:6 where the first conflict with the teachers of the law and Pharisees is described, the beginning of the plans to destroy Jesus' ministry. Compare that episode with this one, which is a result of the earlier confrontation. Word had spread to Jerusalem. Now the group of hostile inquirers is even larger, supplemented by those from Jerusalem who have come to check Jesus out.

The Pharisees were a strong and dominant group within the Jewish religious tradition. Their primary focus was on the law or Torah (the first five books of the Old Testament). However, to the Pharisees the law also included commentaries on the law and how it was to be applied. These commentaries had been created over many generations. The "tradition of the elders" included both Torah and commentary. The teachers of the law are also sometimes called "scribes." They were advisers to the priests and Pharisees.

The issue raised by the Pharisees is not personal hygiene, having hands clean of germs (unknown in their time). The issue is the sanctity of certain foods and the necessity of cleansing one's self from evil before receiving these foods, as the Jewish tradition decreed.

❏ *Mark 7:6-13.* Jesus draws on two Old Testament sources in his response to their accusations since this was important to them: one from the Prophets and one from the Law. The passage from Isaiah identifies a major concern of the prophets, often addressed by them. This concern is over ritual acts of worship that did not represent a commitment of life to God's purposes or even an awareness of what those purposes were. Indeed, the acts had become a substitute for sincerity.

The commandment of Moses (verse 10) called for the honoring of parents that was, and is, a time-honored priority in Jewish religious and family life. However, the offering of possessions to God in a ritual took precedence over using those items to meet basic needs that a parent might have. Suppose some food items had been set aside to be offered to God in a sacrifice. Meanwhile a famine occurred, and their parents had nothing to eat. Under the tradition, the parents could not be given these reserved food items for their survival. The original purpose of the law, to testify to the worth of parents, was overlooked and even contradicted by the refusal of the children to share these items held in reserve.

Tradition becomes not only more important but even cancels out God's intentions. Is it possible that some of our religious traditions or traditional religious viewpoints do that today?

❏ *Mark 7:14-23.* Jesus is commenting on the issue of eating that which is ceremonially unclean. Jesus' primary concern is evident again—the value and worth of persons and what enhances that value. Food items do not determine a person's value. Whether eaten with washed or unwashed hands, those items enter into and leave the body. The quality of a person is made neither better nor worse by those items. A person's quality of being is greatly determined by what is created within a person. From a person's heart cleanliness or lack of it is determined.

Note Mark's comment in verse 19. Mark sees in this the principle that all foods are now to be seen as ritually clean and available to all. This verse is probably included because, at the time Mark was writing, a controversy had arisen in the early church over whether such Jewish laws had to be obeyed by Christians.

❑ *Mark 7:24-30.* Again Jesus is on the move. This time he goes to what is now the lower part of Lebanon. When the Greek woman falls down at Jesus' feet, Mark sees more than simply another desperate person asking for Jesus' healing help. The woman is of Greek background and is living in Phoenicia—she is a non-Jew. Jesus' ministry had begun in Jewish synagogues and had always been to Jewish persons. In his response in which he speaks of first feeding the "children," Jesus acknowledges a prior sense of mission to the children of his tradition and heritage. However, in his response to her insistent pleading for her child, Jesus demonstrated a ministry of caring for all persons.

❑ *Mark 7:31-35.* Jesus returns to the area of the Decapolis (ten cities) around the southern part of the Sea of Galilee. He continues there his healing ministry, again reflecting his concern over the physical well-being of persons and his support of the forces that work for health, not illnesses, within persons. The word *ephphatha* is simply the Aramaic word that would be used in ordinary conversation. Aramaic, a form of Hebrew, was the language used in Jesus' day by Jews in Palestine.

❑ *Mark 7:36-37.* Several times already in Mark we have noticed an attempt on the part of Jesus to keep in private any comments made in tribute to him or about marvelous deeds done by him. There is more to this attempt than simple humility. In Mark, Jesus seems to seek to avoid or withdraw from moments of public acclaim (7:24). He is portrayed as wanting to avoid a general awareness of who he is. For Mark it appeared that Jesus wanted to wait until a certain time late in his ministry before he made a public acknowledgment of his divine personhood.

So Mark's account has an element of suspense to see when this public event will be.

DIMENSION THREE:
WHAT DOES THE BIBLE MEAN TO ME?

Genuine Discipleship in Old Traditions

All of us who are followers of Jesus and inheritors of the traditions of other followers have mixed feelings in relating ourselves to new days and new ways. At times we almost feel like we shall betray our faith if we change our minds or accept a new idea. Often the church has encouraged us to think this way. The church has preserved the faith from the past for us and warned us against being swept away "by every wind of teaching" (Ephesians 4:14). Sometimes following tradition results in the creation of a fortress mentality. Instead of seeing Christian experience as a pilgrimage to exciting new discoveries of God's grace, truth, and power, we see it as a fort to be defended in which we hide, stagnate, and die.

Jesus, in his confrontations with the teachers of the law and Pharisees, wants us to distinguish between the forms of truth and the essence of truth. He wants us to go beneath inherited, traditional forms for the conveyance of spiritual truth to the undying essence of spiritual truth. Finding that essence, Jesus would have us discover anew its application in our day and new forms of expressing it. Jesus is reported as doing this several times in the Gospels. Especially is this apparent in the Sermon on the Mount (Matthew 5–7, especially 5:17-48). There Jesus states that he has not "come to abolish the Law . . . but to fulfill them" (5:17).

God through the Spirit has revealed truth. God through the Spirit is still revealing truth. The Bible is both a sourcebook and a workbook for the discovery of God's truth. The Bible unveils truth, but also guides and prods us to seek more truth and to be open to it.

This chapter also bids us beware of making our walk with Christ a narrow, judgmental walk. We who have known Christ's grace and love, who have received Christ's redemp-

50   MARK

tive therapies in spite of or because of who and what we are, should be the most open to all, sharing the graciousness we have received from Christ. Who is the Syrophoenician woman in our neighborhood with whom we should share what we know and have?

This chapter warns us that we should beware of falling anew into the age-old trap of allowing forms to substitute for genuineness of discipleship, or even to hide away God's purposes and priorities for God's people. We must ever avoid allowing our faith experience to be hardened into ritual acts and encrusted by laws that ultimately will destroy its truth and value.

"But what about you?" he asked. "Who do you say I am?"
Peter answered, "You are the Christ" (8:29).

——— 7 ———

The Tide Begins to Turn
Mark 8:1–9:1

DIMENSION ONE:
WHAT DOES THE BIBLE SAY?

Answer these questions by reading Mark 8:1–9:1

1. What is the problem faced by the crowd? (8:1)

   They had nothing to eat

2. What is the attitude of Jesus toward this crowd? (8:2-3)

   He had compassion on them.

3. What do the disciples ask of Jesus? (8:4)

   Where could they get bread in the wilderness?

4. What does Jesus ask of the disciples in response? What is their answer? (8:5)

   He asked them how many loaves of bread they had

   They said - seven

   and a few small fish

5. Now what does Jesus do? (8:6-7)

He had them to sit on the ground. Then he blessed the bread and fish and the disciples gave to the people

6. What is the result? (8:8)

They all ate and were filled and took up of fragments 7 buckets full

7. How many persons are present? (8:9)

About 4,000.

8. Where does Jesus go? (8:10)

He and his disciples took a ship to Dalmanutha.

9. Who begins to question Jesus? Why? (8:11)

The Pharisees. To Tempt Him to show them a sign.

10. What sign does Jesus give them? (8:12)

He said no sign will be given to them

11. What do the disciples forget to bring with them? (8:14)

They forgot to bring bread.

12. What warning does Jesus give them? (8:15)

He said to beware the leaven of the Pharisees

13. What accusation does Jesus make of his disciples? (8:17-18)

That they could not yet understand

14. What episodes does Jesus have them recall? (8:19-20)

When He fed the 5,000 men with 5 loaves of bread and that they had 12 baskets left over and

15. Whom does Jesus meet next? What is his request? (8:22)

16. What does Jesus do? (8:23, 25)

17. What are the results? (8:24-25)

18. Where does Jesus send the blind man after his sight is restored? (8:26)

19. What questions does Jesus ask of his disciples? (8:27, 29)

20. What are their responses? (8:28-29)

21. What new teaching about himself does Jesus offer his disciples? (8:31)

22. What is Peter's reaction to this news? What is Jesus' reaction to Peter? (8:32-33)

23. What invitation does Jesus extend to the multitude? What will result from accepting it? (8:34-37)

24. Of whom will the Son of Man be ashamed? (8:38)

Those who are ashamed of Him or His word.

25. What prediction does Jesus make? (9:1)

That some of them would not die before seeing the Kingdom of God come with power.

DIMENSION TWO: WHAT DOES THE BIBLE MEAN?

Jesus continues to move successfully in ministry. Crowds are drawn to him, while the disciples are still, at times, puzzled by him. Yet as Jesus reaches the heights of achievement and acclaim, even being seen as the Messiah, the religious leaders against him are becoming more intentional and obvious. Dark forebodings are shared by Jesus with his followers with the understanding that discipleship has a price.

❏ *Mark 8:1-9.* Mark reports a second event involving the feeding of a multitude through Jesus' action. The first, commonly known as the feeding of the five thousand, appeared in 6:35-44. This episode is commonly known as the feeding of the four thousand. You might be interested in comparing the two events, noting their similarities and differences. You may wish to read again the comments on the earlier event in Lesson 5. This second event appears only in Mark and Matthew (15:32-38). For Mark to have included two such events in the short scope of his book must indicate the importance of them to what Mark wanted to stress. What do you think he wanted to stress? This story begins with a reference to the compassion of Jesus for people and their physical as well as spiritual needs. This part of Jesus' nature is repeatedly unveiled by Mark.

In this story we see anew the importance of bread to the common life of the Jewish people. It was, indeed, the "staff of life." Although they had no scientific concept of the fact that bread contains essential vitamins and minerals for the well-being of one's body, they somehow sensed it was valuable to one's strength and health. Thus bread came to have spiritual significance as a symbol of God's providence to meet our physical needs and later of God's presence to meet our spiritual needs. Here in Mark's account the bread does not appear to have any special symbolism of the bread beyond being the expression of God's providence, as enabled by Jesus, expanding to meet the physical needs of people.

The presence of this large crowd, as well as the preceding event in which a deaf and speechless person was brought to Jesus (7:32), may possibly be attributed to the witness made by "Legion." In this same area of the Decapolis, Legion had been met by Jesus and healed of his mental torment. Jesus had told him to tell his friends what God had done for him. This the man did throughout this area (5:19-20). What an impact one person's witness can have!

❏ *Mark 8:10.* The exact size and location of Dalmanutha is unknown. It is thought to have been in the area of Magdala on the western shore of the Sea of Galilee.

❏ *Mark 8:11-13.* You may wish to recall the earlier confrontations of Jesus with the Pharisees (2:18-28; 7:1-13) and the material on them in Lessons 2 and 6. In the earlier events the Pharisees are critical of the lifestyle of the disciples and Jesus as failing to show obedience to the law. Now they turn to another tactic, seeking to trip up Jesus. They call on him to provide some sign from heaven to prove who he is. If Jesus cannot do this, as they expect, it will prove he has no special relationship with God.

In the Old Testament *signs* were looked on, or looked for, as evidence of God's blessings or empowerment. Out of this tradition the Pharisees call for signs. Once again Jesus will not use the miraculous for selfish purposes.

❑ *Mark 8:14-21.* Still pondering his conversation with the Pharisees, Jesus senses their growing opposition and willingness to use any methods to undermine him. So he warns his disciples that even they may be subject to the Pharisees' influence (like leaven that, unseen, changes dough). For the third time the disciples are anxious about food (see 6:35-36 and 8:4). By recalling what has happened previously, Jesus is trying to shift their focus from their need to God's providence. Jesus' teaching ministry, feeding the four thousand, feeding the five thousand, and walking on the water are overshadowed by the blindness of the disciples.

❑ *Mark 8:22-26.* The story in these verses is similar to the story reported in 7:32-37. The healing act is the touch of Jesus upon the blind man. His restored vision is blurred at first as he sees persons "like trees walking around." Gradually his vision clears. Mark places this story before Jesus reveals Jesus' secret (8:27-30). This story suggests Jesus alone can open the eyes of the blind through faith. Is there not a sense in which all of us find ourselves able, slowly but surely, to see persons more clearly after the touch of Jesus on our lives?

❑ *Mark 8:27-30.* Caesarea Philippi is located about thirty miles north of Bethsaida and the Sea of Galilee. In response to Jesus' inquiry, the disciples convey the oft-heard explanations as to his identity. These were also mentioned earlier (6:14-15). (Refer to the commentary on those verses in Lesson 5.) Peter affirms that Jesus is the Christ (the Messiah, the Anointed One). Jesus still wants this information held in confidence.

❑ *Mark 8:31-33. Son of Man* is a term with roots in the Old Testament. The phrase is ultimately used for a special person, a triumphant servant of God, as described in Daniel 7:13. By using this title for himself, Jesus gives it a new meaning. Instead of being aloof and triumphantly superior, the Son of Man as modeled by Jesus becomes, indeed, the son (or servant) of humankind. This model will be expressed through rejection and suffering, even to death. But God will vindicate Jesus by enabling him to be raised from the dead.

Peter has an entirely different concept of the Christ, thinking of such as victor and ruler, which was the traditional expectation of the Messiah. Jesus tells Peter bluntly that Peter is more in tune with human desire than with God's purposes. ❏ *Mark 8:34–9:1.* Jesus opens up his invitation. Now it is not just to a select few but to all who will hear him. Anyone may come with Jesus, but they cannot expect their lot to be different from his. They will have to deny some of their natural human desires for convenience and comfort. They will find their own cross. They should keep their focus on Jesus. The result of momentary hesitation to pay this price to accept Jesus' invitation is ultimate embarrassment at the time of his triumph. For some who seriously accept the invitation and pay the price, they will experience the presence of God in their lives as King in this life, not having to wait until after death.

DIMENSION THREE:
WHAT DOES THE BIBLE MEAN TO ME?

Mark 8:34–9:1—Triumph and Tragedy

This chapter brings us the picture of triumph and tragedy as the two rhythms in the life of Jesus. Jesus has had an amazing ministry to the multitudes as well as to individuals and his disciples. Yet the tragedy of spiritual blindness and immaturity, the plotting against him, and the dismal predictions of worse to come are all around Jesus. The thrilling confession of Peter that Jesus is the Christ and the costly invitation of Jesus to whomever will walk in self-surrender to follow him form the crescendo in the middle of Mark's narrative. The cymbals crash at the moment of Peter's confession; but the solemn, hushed notes of the cello immediately follow as Jesus outlines what it will mean to be Son of Man. Yet he daringly invites us to join him. What is the cause of the conflict between Peter and Jesus?

Contrary to what we often think, the cross that Jesus invites us to take up is not forced on us. Our cross is not life's misfortunes: illness, responsibility for others, physical handicaps, limited resources. Rather, the cross of which Jesus speaks is one we take up. We could avoid it; we do not have to bear it. Yet in spite of that option we walk over to where it is; on our own volition we pick it up; and then we carry it. Our cross is personal, uniquely suited to our own distaste. It hurts me; it involves a sacrifice by me; it is carried by me because of what it can mean to someone else. Yet the cross is the way redemption comes to me and others.

*As they were coming down the mountain, Jesus gave them
orders not to tell anyone what they had seen until the Son of
Man had risen from the dead (9:9).*

—— 8 ——

Down From the Mountain
Mark 9:2-50

DIMENSION ONE:
WHAT DOES THE BIBLE SAY?

Answer these questions by reading Mark 9:2-50

1. Where does Jesus go? Whom does he take with him? (9:2)

   Mountain top, Taking Peter, James and John

2. What happens there? Who also joins them? (9:2-4)

   *Jesus face shone with glory and his clothing very white
   Elijah and Moses appeared
   (Elias)*

3. What is the reaction of these three disciples, especially
   Peter? (9:5-6)

   *They were very afraid
   Peter wanted to make three tabernacles — one for Jesus
   one for Moses
   one for Elias*

4. What event then takes place? (9:7)

   The Transfiguration

5. What order does Jesus give the three disciples as they come down from the mountain? What do they do? (9:9-10)

6. As a follow-up to the Transfiguration experience, what question do these disciples ask Jesus? (9:11)

7. What is Jesus' answer? (9:12-13)

8. On returning from the mountain, what do Jesus, Peter, James, and John find the rest of the disciples doing? (9:14-18)

9. What does Jesus say? (9:19)

10. What request does the father of the ill boy make of Jesus? (9:21b-22)

11. What promise does Jesus offer? What unusual prayer is offered by the father in response? (9:23-24)

12. What happens when Jesus seeks to eliminate the evil spirit? (9:25-27)

13. What question do the disciples ask of Jesus? What is his response? (9:28-29)

14. What teaching does Jesus repeat to his disciples that they still do not understand? (9:30-32)

15. What do the disciples discuss together that they do not want to admit to Jesus? (9:33-34)

16. What counsel does Jesus give them? (9:35)

17. How does a child enter the story at this point? (9:36-37)

18. What does John report to Jesus? (9:38)

19. What new understanding does Jesus give the disciples? (9:39-40)

20. How does Jesus use a cup of water? (9:41)

21. What warning does Jesus give to anyone who causes "little ones" who believe in him to sin? (9:42)

22. What harsh advice does Jesus give? (9:43-48)

23. How does Jesus use salt in his teaching? (9:50)

DIMENSION TWO:
WHAT DOES THE BIBLE MEAN?

In this lesson we come to the "mountain-top experience." This particular story from Jesus' life gives us that phrase. The experience is filled with drama and significance that defies our complete understanding. Yet part of the story is also the trip back—the blending of inspiration and perspiration, or heavenliness and earthliness. This event is the pinnacle in the middle of Mark's story from which the journey into the valley of the shadow of death will take place.

❏ *Mark 9:2-8*. Although the designation of a gap of "six days" could just be for information, possibly "six days" is mentioned to suggest that this high event of genuine worship takes place on the sabbath.

Peter, James, and John now form an inner circle or executive group of the disciples. Note their first selection by Jesus (5:37) to be part of a highly dramatic and unusual experience. Note also the prediction of Jesus at the close of our last lesson in 9:1. Possibly that verse is intentionally included to be a bridge to the Transfiguration experience. To Mark the awareness of God's presence and voice, the return of Moses and Elijah, and the transformed appearance of Jesus may be in impressiveness, if not in fact, "the kingdom of God come with power" (9:1).

The site of the Transfiguration is unknown. A hillside overlooking the Sea of Galilee on the northern shore traditionally has been regarded as the site. Some scholars think it took place farther north near Mount Hermon. Jesus is "transfigured," not transformed. His appearance is different. The difference may refer to the fact that because of what took place, the disciples saw Jesus in a different light. The Transfiguration becomes a visible confirmation to them of what Peter affirmed in 8:29. Before this event, the disciples had seen Jesus as a prophet and had pondered that it might be possible he was Messiah and God's Son. At this experience they see the marks of divinity shine and the status of Messiah confirmed. Thus, the disciples will never see Jesus quite the same again. He will always be "transfigured" to their perceptions.

The "shelters" of which Peter speaks are intended to be temporary. Judging from what is said in verse 6, this suggestion was an impulsive outburst in the midst of the emotion of the moment. Peter wanted to extend what was taking place so that it would not abruptly end.

Probably this entire mountaintop happening was intended to be seen as a "new Moses" upon a "new Sinai." The presence of Moses, the great Lawgiver in Jewish tradition (Exodus 19), with Jesus implies that Jesus is on equal ground with Moses and has God's sanction to be the new Lawgiver ("This is my Son, whom I love. Listen to him!" verse 7). Furthermore, the presence of Elijah (see the commentaries in earlier lessons on 6:15 and 8:28), regarded as the first of the prophets, implies Jesus is in the prophetic tradition, indeed, the greatest of the prophets as Messiah.

❏ *Mark 9:9-10.* Surprisingly after such an event as the Transfiguration Jesus still insists that no one be told "what they had seen." However, this statement is consistent with the attitude of Jesus previously reported in Mark (3:12; 5:43; 7:36; 8:30). The messianic secret still prevails until Jesus decrees it is to be unveiled. When do you think that will be? Is the answer in verse 10?

❏ *Mark 9:11-13, 30-32.* Verses 11-13 are puzzling. Again the reference to Elijah suggests how strong was the tradition of his return prior to the Messiah. The expectation was that he would get everything "straightened out" for the Messiah's coming. Thus the disciples cannot understand why Jesus talks of having to suffer. In effect, Jesus says in another way that being God's servant for a special task does not provide immunity from trouble. It was not true of Elijah (or John the Baptist) and will not be true of Jesus.

Note that Jesus continues to use "Son of Man" as he refers to himself, especially in the context of his future suffering.

❏ *Mark 9:14-19.* The inspiration is over, the perspiration begins. Jesus is confronted again with crowds, dissension, and spiritual inadequacy. His patience is tried and brings him to the verge of disgust, as expressed in verse 19. Jesus gives priority to meeting the child's need rather than be drawn into arguments about the child's need. The problem is that of epilepsy as indicated by the symptoms described in verses 18 and 22. Each attack created a comatose condition. These attacks have even resulted in his collapsing into fires or bodies of water if the young man was standing near them. The damage of the disease is made worse by wounds resulting from falls.

At the center of this story is the divine promise and the human touch. Jesus describes belief (a faith that is deep enough to issue forth in action) as the pathway to unlimited possibilities. The father responds by acknowledging that he does have a measure of faith but needs help to overcome the pockets of disbelief that lurk within himself (verse 24). Have you experienced moments in your life when you were confronted with a demand or need so large that this was your prayer? Take courage—for Jesus is drawn to the side of those human enough to know their inadequacies but willing enough to experience new possibilities through his outreach. After another convulsion occurs, Jesus "took him by the hand and lifted him to his feet" (verse 27).

Jesus indicates to the disciples who had failed to be of help that only through prayer could genuine and lasting help be imparted to a person in desperate need. The disciples may have been relying on their spiritual status as companions of Jesus or their spiritual showmanship. No, Jesus cautions. Therapeutic spiritual help can only be provided when one knows he or she does not have it to give. Then in dependent desperation they turn to God "who is able to do immeasurably more than all we ask or imagine, according to his power that is at work within us" (Ephesians 3:20).

❑ *Mark 9:31-37, 42-50.* The discussion among the disciples as to who is the greatest may have arisen out of the Transfiguration experience. Were Peter, James, and John now the greatest because of what they alone had witnessed with Jesus? Does special spiritual experience create spiritual superiority? To these ideas Jesus responds with a child as centerpiece. The child may be the least noticed but is of the most value. The child may not be considered the most important family member, but by their parenting priority, a couple may make a child become that important. We do not find our spiritual value by virtue or demand or chance, only by our awareness of need and our openness to God.

Thus, our relationship to each other is to be that which assists others to find and keep value in life. Anything we do to lessen or destroy values in others is a violation of why we have each other. It destroys us even more than it damages the other person.

66   MARK

In this passage Mark first uses the word translated "hell." This word is *gehenna* and was the name of an area in the Valley of Hinnom located just outside the old city walls of Jerusalem. At this place the trash of the city was deposited and burned. The fires usually burned continuously. From this you can see where the common images of hell (a lower world with everlasting fire for the punishment of wicked persons) originated. Additionally, Matthew and Luke use a second word in some passages, *Hades* (Matthew 11:23; 16:18; Luke 10:15; 16:23). *Hades* is the exact Greek word given English letters and means an unseen world. While both words refer to a realm in the afterlife reserved for the dead, they are not the same word.

No sacrifice is too great to avoid a destructive spiritual influence, which ultimately will destroy us. Can you recall illustrations from your life?

DIMENSION THREE:
WHAT DOES THE BIBLE MEAN TO ME?

Inspirational Experiences

The affirmation of Jesus as the Christ takes place in Mark 8. Immediately Jesus describes his probable sufferings and death as a servant of God's purposes. The Transfiguration of Jesus to confirm that he is the Christ takes place in Chapter 9. Immediately Jesus enters into controversy, confronts lifelong physical illness, deals with self-seeking disciples, and warns against the potential for self-destruction in one's damaging influence on others.

In both chapters, the feelings from the dramatic episodes of revelation and inspiration are plowed by Jesus into the furrows of human need. Jesus refuses to accept acclaim but feels compelled to meet needs. Earthly needs become the arena for expending the energies of divine inspiration.

The disciples ended up frustrated and defeated. They come apart with Jesus and say, "Why, Jesus? We have just had the greatest experience in the world. The Lord was there, spiritual heroes of the faith were there, and life was bright and beautiful. Why can't we have it here?" Then Jesus counsels them:

DOWN FROM THE MOUNTAIN **67**

"You cannot boast of your spiritual experiences unless somehow they are transformed into spiritual energy." The inspirational experiences have to recharge the battery. Maybe this is another reason Jesus told them to tell no one what they had seen. First of all, others will not understand the experience. Second, they will think you are bragging. Third, you can make better use of spiritual experiences than talking about them. You can convert them into spiritual energy.

*They were on their way up to Jerusalem,
with Jesus leading the way, and the disciples were astonished,
while those who followed were afraid (10:32).*

— 9 —

On the Road Again

Mark 10

DIMENSION ONE:
WHAT DOES THE BIBLE SAY?

Answer these questions by reading Mark 10

1. Where does Jesus go now? What does he do there? (10:1)

   *When He left Capernaum and went south to Judea border
   and east of Jordan River. He taught the crowd*

2. What questions do the Pharisees and Jesus ask of each
   other? (10:2-4) *The Pharisee tried to trap him by asking
   if He permitted divorce.*

3. What commentary does Jesus make about this law? (10:5-
   9)

4. What additional teaching on this subject does Jesus add
   later for his disciples? (10:10-12)

5. Who are brought to Jesus? What is the disciples' reaction? (10:13)

6. What feeling does Jesus have, and what does he say? (10:14-15)

7. What does Jesus do with the children? (10:16)

Put His hands upon them and blessed them

8. What question is asked by the man who runs to meet Jesus? (10:17)

Good master, what shall I do that I may inherit eternal life?

9. What answer does Jesus give? (10:18-19)

10. What is the man's reaction and Jesus' advice? (10:20-21)

11. What are the inner feelings of the man and of Jesus? (10:21-22)

12. What commentary does Jesus make about rich persons? (10:23-25)

    He said "How hardly shalt they that have riches enter into the Kingdom of God!"

13. How do the disciples react to this commentary? (10:24, 26)

    They were astonished, saying "Who then can be saved?"

14. How does Jesus answer them? (10:27)

    "With men it is impossible, but not with God. for with God all things are possible"

15. What is Peter's testimony and Jesus' response? (10:28-31)

16. Where does Jesus now head, leading the disciples? What is their feeling about it? (10:32)

    Jerusalem

17. What does Jesus say awaits him in Jerusalem? (10:33-34)

18. What request do James and John make of Jesus? (10:35-37)

19. What question does Jesus ask them? What is their answer? (10:38-39a)

20. How does Jesus respond to their answer? (10:39b-40)

21. After the other disciples become indignant with James and John, what insight does Jesus give them? (10:42-45)

22. To what town do they come? Whom do they meet there? (10:46-47)

Jericho
A great number of people and a blind man

23. What is the reaction of the crowd and of Jesus to Bartimaeus? (10:48-49)

They rebuked him but Jesus called him to Him

24. What does Jesus ask him? What is Bartimaeus's request? (10:51)

"What can I do for you?"
"That I may receive my sight"
He received his sight and followed Jesus

DIMENSION TWO:
WHAT DOES THE BIBLE MEAN?

Mark 10 records the transition of the ministry of Jesus from the northern areas of Palestine to the southern areas. The chapter tells of events that took place on the journey south. However, this transition marks more than a change in place. The transition marks a change to a new phase of Jesus' ministry. Jerusalem, to which Jesus now heads, will be the place of supreme testing and final hours. As Jesus moves south, Jesus knows this testing is facing him—and those with him sense it too.

❏ *Mark 10:1, 46.* In the previous chapter Jesus made his last tour of ministry in Galilee, probably making his last visits to the area where he grew up, in and around Nazareth. Jesus alone may have sensed that this trip was his last visit home.

After returning to Capernaum for a last visit, Jesus travels south across the Sea of Galilee. Then probably he and his disciples travel south in the vicinity of the Jordan River. The Jordan flows directly south from the Sea of Galilee about sixty-five miles (if it went in a straight line) to the Dead Sea. East of the Jordan, commonly called "across the Jordan" or Transjordan, was the province of Perea (now part of the country of Jordan). West of the river were the provinces of Samaria and Judea, where Jerusalem was located. Jesus goes south on a route taking him on both sides of the Jordan until he reaches Jericho.

❏ *Mark 10:2-12.* Again the Pharisees put Jesus to the test by asking him whether divorce is lawful. Jesus asks them to recall the law of Moses on this subject as stated in Deuteronomy 24:1-4. This law provided that if a husband found something "indecent" about his wife, he could simply write out a statement of divorce and send her away. Someone else could then marry her. The only thing prohibited was for a previous husband to remarry a woman. This law gave privilege to the man and no protection to the woman.

In Mark's account Jesus views permission for divorce in the law as an unfortunate concession to human weakness and indifference to God's intentions for marriage. Drawing on the creation of woman and man and marriage as stated in Genesis 1:27 and 2:24, Jesus sees the two persons as becoming "one flesh." This oneness does not allow for a husband to dismiss (or divorce) his wife. Jesus goes further by disavowing the law's provision for second or more marriages for the divorced.

Beneath what comes across as a negative and restrictive interpretation by Jesus is something positive—a new pioneering support for the value of women as persons, rather than possessions, and their entitlement to certain rights as persons. This valuing of women ran counter to the culture of the day, which was patriarchal and saw women as little more than property.

❑ *Mark 10:13-16.* Having affirmed the importance of marriage stability, now Jesus has an occasion to affirm the value of children. Bringing children to an honored rabbi for his blessing would be a frequent desire for Jewish mothers. In the same spirit these mothers came with children to Jesus for his blessing ("to have him touch them"). Jesus' response to the rejection of these mothers by the disciples is that of grieving resentment. This feeling was surely enhanced by the awareness that he had recently witnessed to his disciples about the importance of children, saying that to receive a child was to receive him (9:33-37). In spite of this, they still reject the children.

Now Jesus identifies children as a model of the kingdom of God.

❑ *Mark 10:17-22.* With eagerness or a deep sense of need, a man runs up to Jesus asking how to "inherit eternal life." This man is usually identified as the rich young ruler because Matthew writes of him as a young man (Matthew 19:22). Mark gives us no information as to the man's age. His admiration of Jesus is evidenced by his calling Jesus "good teacher." Jesus uses his customary style of answering a question with a question. Jesus rejects the man's word, responding that only God is good. This answer typifies the profound sense of reverence in which God was held in Jewish tradition. God was seen as the sum of all that is righteous and just. God is goodness.

Jesus recalls the traditional view that obedience to the law is the pathway to life. And Jesus, as usual, does not overthrow the value of the law but goes beyond it to something even more basic. The essence of commitment, even to the law, is the offering of the self as a living sacrifice to that principle. Now Jesus points out that what is needed is the offering of self to persons, who are even more important than principles. There must be a moving out from self in Jesus' name and spirit to meet the needs of others. Because his priorities would have to change, the man goes away "sad."

❑ *Mark 10:23-31.* In various ways Jesus has overthrown the usual perspectives. He does it again. The prevailing attitude was that obedience led to life and that possessions were the blessings of God for obedience. Now Jesus points to a new kind of obedience that leads to life: the sacrifice of self and possessions. Recognizing this to be contrary to what happens, the disciples wonder whether anyone can be saved. Jesus says that if persons depend on their own efforts at obedience or goodness it is not possible. Salvation is possible when God by grace opens the door, and God's Spirit within us enables us to go through the door.

Discovering that sacrifice is the key to the Kingdom. Peter boasts of the sacrifice of the disciples. Jesus implies that "life" will be theirs, but "life" is not to be equated with comfort.

❑ *Mark 10:32-34.* They move closer to Jerusalem. Jesus leads the way. He restates what lies ahead for him in Jerusalem in more specific terms. The disciples feel a growing anxiety and an increasing puzzlement that if Jesus is correct as to what awaits him, then why does he continue on to Jerusalem? Yet Jesus still leads the way.

❑ *Mark 10:35-45.* Perhaps James and John now accept the bitter truth that Jesus may be at the beginning of the end. This belief may lie behind their seemingly vain request to be at the right and left of Jesus in his glory.

Jesus uses the words *cup* and *baptized* in a figurative sense. (See Mark 14:36.) These words refer to the cup of suffering and the baptism of unfortunate circumstances. These will be the disciples' lot, as they will be for Jesus too. He cannot promise them glory, for glory is not in the job description for the followers of Jesus. He can only promise them service.

❑ *Mark 10:46-52.* When Jesus and the disciples come to Jericho, they are only about seventeen miles from Jerusalem, at the beginning of the steep winding road that climbs through the arid wilderness to Mount Zion. Crowds continue to surround Jesus as he enters the last phase of his journey. Yet again a person's need causes Jesus to pause on the way. Just as the disciples did to the parents bringing the children, so the crowd acts to the blind man ("many rebuked him"). Jesus acts differently. He calls Bartimaeus to his side, listens to his need, and responds. Bartimaeus responds by following Jesus into Jerusalem.

DIMENSION THREE:
WHAT DOES THE BIBLE MEAN TO ME?

The New Road With Jesus

As you look back over this chapter, you could end up with a hopeless feeling about the possibilities of discipleship for you. In this chapter we read of high, almost rigid, expectations for permanence in marriage and avoidance of remarriage. We hear a call for obedience to the primary commandments. We receive a summons to shed all we have and share with the poor. We are to leave all and follow Jesus. Then Jesus warns that to have many possessions may even block our entrance into the Kingdom. The prediction for disciples is that their lot may be the same as the lot for Jesus: service, suffering, and even death.

Lest this leave us completely overwhelmed with a paralyzing sense of inadequacy, we must see this all in perspective. As Jesus walked ahead of them on the demanding roadway (10:32), so Jesus always walks ahead of us on the road of discipleship. He would lead us into relationships that are taken seriously and preserved, into a respect for children and the simplicities of faith they symbolize, into a lifestyle of giving and sharing rather than getting and grandstanding, from the model of a master to that of a servant. At more than one point everyone of us will fall by the wayside. But Jesus hears the hurts of those by the wayside. We will, like Bartimaeus, cry for mercy. We can take heart because he will stop for us.

Then with Jesus' gracious understanding undergirding us and the renewed sight he shall give us, we can follow him.

*Those who went ahead and those who followed shouted,
"Hosanna!" / "Blessed is he who comes in the name of the
Lord!" (11:9).*

— 10 —
Is This the Holy City?
Mark 11:1–12:12

DIMENSION ONE:
WHAT DOES THE BIBLE SAY?

Answer these questions by reading Mark 11:1-25

1. Where do Jesus and the disciples come? (11:1)

2. What directions does Jesus give two of his disciples? (11:2-3)

3. What happens when the disciples go on their errand? (11:4-6)

4. What is done with the colt? (11:7-8)

5. What do the crowds do? (11:8-10)

6. What does Jesus do in Jerusalem? (11:11)

7. What object does Jesus notice that prompts him to comment in an unusual fashion? (11:12-14)

8. What dramatic event takes place when Jesus returns to Jerusalem? (11:15-17)

9. What Old Testament passage does Jesus quote? (11:17)

10. What is the reaction of the religious leaders? (11:18)

11. What new discovery is made as the fig tree is seen again? (11:20-21)

12. What counsel and promise does Jesus make? (11:22-23)

13. What guidance does Jesus offer about prayer? (11:24-26)

Answer these questions by reading Mark 11:27–12:12

14. Who are the religious leaders who approach Jesus? (11:27) What questions do they ask him? (11:28)

15. What question does Jesus ask in response? (11:30)

16. What argument among them does Jesus' question create? (11:31-32)

17. What does the discussion conclude? (11:33)

18. What form of teaching does Jesus use again? (12:1a)

Parables (stories)

19. What does the owner of the vineyard do? (12:1b-2)

20. What reception is given to these servants? (12:3-5)

21. What does the owner do? (12:6)

    He sent his only Son.

22. What is the tenants' action? (12:7-8) What is the owner's
    reaction? (12:9)

    They decided to kill the Son and inherit the vineyard

    He killed the wicked workers

23. What Old Testament passage does Jesus quote? (12:10-11)

    The cornerstone rejected by the builders

    became the Cornerstone

24. What do the religious leaders do? (12:12)

    They wanted to arrest Jesus
    but they were afraid to
    So they left

DIMENSION TWO:
WHAT DOES THE BIBLE MEAN?

Humanity and divinity are reflected in the triumphal entry
and what follows, both within and around Jesus. Indeed,
divinity and humanity confront each other directly in the Holy
City. This plot unfolds in Mark 11 and 12.

❑ *Mark 11:1.* Jesus walks up the Jericho road. The trip is about seventeen miles long. Mark leaves the impression that Jesus had not visited Jerusalem before. Luke tells of a childhood visit of Jesus in the Temple at Jerusalem (Luke 2:41-50). John tells of several earlier visits to Jerusalem (John 2:13; 5:1; 7:10). Obviously, Jesus has some familiarity already with the city. Pilgrims to the Passover festival would often stay in these villages when the city was crowded. Bethany is on the side of the Mount of Olives.

❑ *Mark 11:2-6.* As Jesus gives directions, he appears to be familiar with the area. Also it appears that he had followers there, judging from their willingness to provide immediately if "the Lord needs it." The colt was a donkey colt. In choosing this form of entry Jesus chooses an expression of humility, which is in keeping with Mark's portrait of Jesus. Also it fulfills a prophecy of humble entrance by the Messiah found in Zechariah 9:9.

❑ *Mark 11:7-10.* The garments were thrown on the colt to be a form of saddle for Jesus' comfort. The spreading of garments and branches on the roadway is a form of tribute usually reserved for rulers and popular heroes. It is like spreading the red carpet. *Hosanna* means "O save" or "Save now." The crowds are shouting, or more probably singing or chanting, words from Psalm 118:26, which was used to refer to the Messiah. The reference to the "coming kingdom of our father David" is also a reference to the Messiah. The Messiah was to come from the line of David. Thus the cries of the crowd are their acknowledgment that Jesus is indeed the Messiah.

❑ *Mark 11:11.* When Matthew and Luke wrote their accounts based on Mark's account, they located the cleansing of the Temple at this point. However, in Mark's account Jesus looks around the Temple and becomes personally aware of the situation there. Jesus and the disciples return to the village of Bethany for the night.

❑ *Mark 11:12-14, 20-25.* These verses tell of a puzzling event that seems out of character with Jesus. New Testament scholars have gone in several directions to try to explain this episode. Your teacher may point out some of these explanations.

The odd feature of the story is that Jesus seeks to find figs on a tree when figs are not in season. An early fig reportedly grew on some trees. Perhaps Jesus was seeking this fig. The first part of the story when the tree is condemned to be fruitless occurs on Monday as the disciples and Jesus are en route to the Temple. The second part when the tree is seen withered occurs on Tuesday morning. One possible interpretation is to see Jesus acting as a prophet, which he would also do later in the day in the Temple and later in the week with warnings about the future. Sometimes prophets engaged in prophetic acts. The fruitful tree was a traditional symbol of Israel and the servant of God. To fail to produce spiritual fruit was to fail in God's purpose for them. Jesus may have been showing how God looked in vain for true spiritual fruit from Israel. Having failed in their calling, they have lost their future and merit God's judgment. This interpretation needs to be seen in connection with the cleansing of the Temple.

❑ *Mark 11:15-19.* This unusual act by Jesus is reported in all four Gospels. Obviously, it made a lasting impression on people. The acclaim Jesus had received the previous day is the foundation of support needed by Jesus to dare to carry out such an act of civil disobedience.

The items for sale in the Temple primarily would be animals for ritual sacrificial offerings, including pigeons that were a permissible sacrifice for the poor who could not afford lambs. The "money changers" would enable travelers who came to the Temple from distant places to change their money into the local currency to use to purchase animals for offerings. Corruption and unfair dealings may have been involved in these commercial activities taking place within the Temple. The statement of Jesus in verse 17 is a combination of two Old Testament passages: Isaiah 56:7 and Jeremiah 7:11.

This act of repudiation of common Temple practices, which undoubtedly brought income to the Temple rulers was a direct attack on the policies of the religious leaders, the "chief priests and the teachers of the law."

❑ *Mark 11:27-33.* The struggle of this passage is similar to those at the beginning of Jesus' ministry (2:1–3:6). Jesus dares to come to the Temple. Immediately Jesus was accosted by the religious leaders. Note that this time the chief priests and teachers of the law are accompanied by the "elders" (verse 27). The elders were members of the policy-making Sanhedrin who would be called on to try Jesus. The leaders want the elders to observe Jesus and thus sensitize them to what needs to be addressed—to get them ready to endorse what the religious leaders will propose. They are hoping to trap Jesus into stating he is the Messiah as they ask him about his authority. This would bring the charge of blasphemy. Jesus turns their question around and reveals, by their unwillingness to pass judgment on John the Baptist, that the religious leaders do not act with spiritual authority themselves.

❑ *Mark 12:1-9.* Jesus returns to the use of parable in his teaching. By talking about a vineyard, Jesus talks about a place with which every listener is familiar. Also, *vineyard* is a familiar figure of speech used to represent Israel. So the story can refer to Jesus' listeners in particular and Israel in general. The hedge would serve as a fence to mark borders and keep animals out. The tower would be for protection against destructive animals or thieves.

❑ *Mark 12:10-12.* This quotation comes from the same psalm (118) that was used by the crowds at the triumphal entry. Jesus recalls the psalm and stresses a different portion. The religious leaders see the quotation as applying to them. Now arrest is in the works, although briefly postponed.

DIMENSION THREE:
WHAT DOES THE BIBLE MEAN TO ME?

Bearing Christ

As servants of Christ, we ought to become Christ's colt. At times we bear Christ into moments of triumphant praise in an atmosphere such as Advent and Easter. But there is always Lent, Holy Week, and the way of sorrows. Sometimes Christ moves into unavoidable judgment on self-preserving religious attitudes and traditions that are closed to new light and aloof to the primacy of persons' needs. Here too we must bear Christ. Christ calls us, and we must pay the price. If nothing else, the price to be paid is our willingness to enter with Christ into the arenas of service.

What I say to you, I say to everyone: "Watch!" (13:37).

—— 11 ——
What Does the Future Hold?
Mark 12:13–13:37

**DIMENSION ONE:
WHAT DOES THE BIBLE SAY?**

Answer these questions by reading Mark 12:13-44

1. What new question do the Pharisees and Herodians ask? (12:13-15a)

2. What does Jesus do and say in response? (12:15b-17)

3. What new group comes to Jesus? What question do they ask? (12:18-23)

4. What question does Jesus ask in response to their question? (12:24)

5. Then what answer does Jesus give? (15:25-27)

6. What question does a teacher of the law ask Jesus? (12:28)

7. What two laws does Jesus identify in his answer? (12:29-31)

8. What reaction does the teacher of the law have to Jesus' answer? (12:32-33)

9. What opinion does Jesus have of the teacher of the law? (12:34a)

10. What do the observers hesitate to do? (12:34b)

    They did not dare to ask Him any more questions

11. What question does Jesus ask in the Temple? Why? (12:35-37)

Why do the religious teachers claim the Messiah must be a descendant of King David? Since David called Him his Lord, how could He be his son?

12. What accusations and warning does Jesus include in his teaching? (12:38-40)

Beware of false teachers of religion. They love to wear rich robes and be bowed to and sit in the best seats at banquets. But they shamelessly cheat widows out of their homes. Then they pray long prayers. Their punishment will be greater.

13. Where does Jesus sit down? Whom does he observe there? (12:41-42)

By the collection boxes in the Temple

Some were rich, put in large amounts but a poor widow dropped in two pennies

14. What value does Jesus place on her contribution? (12:43-44)

That she gave more than the rich because she gave all she had. They gave a little of their excess.

Answer these questions by reading Mark 13

15. What impresses one of the disciples? What shocking response does Jesus make? (13:1-2)

The beauty of the Temple. Jesus said not one stone will be left upon another, except as ruin.

16. At the Mount of Olives, with whom does Jesus have a private conversation? What do they ask him? (13:3-4)

Peter, James, John and Andrew
"When is all this to happen?"
"Will there be warning?"

17. As Jesus begins his answer, what warning does he give? (13:5-8)

Do not anymore deceive you

18. What unfortunate events await the disciples of Jesus? (13:9-13)

"Be warned! You will be in danger to be taken before

19. What consolations does Jesus offer? (13:10-13)

20. What event signifies a dangerous era? (13:14)

21. What does Jesus say persons should do when this event does take place? (13:14-16)

22. How does Jesus describe this period? (13:17-20)

23. What warning does Jesus give about false Christs? (13:21-23)

24. What will happen after this tribulation? (13:24-27)

25. When will these things happen? (13:30-32)

DIMENSION TWO:
WHAT DOES THE BIBLE MEAN?

The scriptural material studied in this lesson is in two sections. The first section, 12:13-44, is another round of inquiries between the religious leaders and Jesus. In part the religious leaders are curious about Jesus' answers to questions repeatedly discussed in Jewish religious circles. However, some questions are asked with an intent to trap Jesus. By his answers to questions on controversial issues, they hope to obtain data on the basis of which legal accusations can be brought against Jesus immediately. The second section, Chapter 13, moves beyond the immediate moment to the distant future. Not just Jesus is tested; all humanity will ultimately be tested. Not just Jesus will go to trial; all his followers will experience trial in one way or another.

Issues of great immediate concern and of great ultimate concern are addressed in Mark 12 and 13.

❑ *Mark 12:13-17.* The Herodians were Jews in support of Herod Antipas, the ruler of Galilee and Perea. They wanted Herod to be made ruler of Judea also, which had been made a royal province, subject directly to Rome. Both church and state, so to speak, now approach Jesus "to catch him in his words." Although the issue appears to be taxation, the real issue is whether the Jews owe allegiance to God or to the emperor (the state). Taxation was opposed because it appeared to subject the Jews to Caesar. To answer either way would place Jesus in a position that might result in religious or governmental charges against him.

The coins of the Roman Empire have the image of the ruling Caesar on them. Jesus infers that we have two sets of obligations, both of which must be honored.

❑ *Mark 12:18-27.* The Sadducees are another group within the Jewish religious tradition. The name is traceable to the proper name Zadok, a famous priest. The Sadducees strongly supported the priesthood in Jerusalem. They did not believe in all the additions to the law made by teachers across the years. Thus they are less rigid in their religious outlook and more accommodating to the forces around them.

Since they do not believe in the resurrection, the Sadducees may be asking their question in jest. The question is based on an important Mosaic law found in Deuteronomy 25:5. Jesus turns the question in a different direction. The quotation in verse 26 comes from Exodus 3:6 where God describes God in this way to Moses. Jesus uses the familiar quotation to remind his hearers that God transcends the ordinary human spans of time and relationship.

❑ *Mark 12:28-34.* Now a dialogue begins that has a different flavor from the other conversations with teachers of the law and Pharisees. This teacher of the law, in contrast to the others mentioned by Mark, is favorably impressed by Jesus' answers. The teacher of the law's positive feelings about Jesus prompt him to ask his question about the greatest commandment.

In answering, Jesus gives the expected answer. He quotes Deuteronomy 6:4 known as the Shema (Shee-MAH, the Hebrew word for the first word of that verse: *Hear*), which was used often in family and synagogue worship. But then Jesus adds something unexpected about one's neighbor (Leviticus 19:18). He puts these two together to define the greatest commandment.

This passage is important in Mark because it is the heart of what Mark wants us to learn from Jesus and to see demonstrated by Jesus. The teacher of the law, by agreeing with and expanding on Jesus' answer, shows that he (the teacher of the law) in contrast with other teachers of the law, now believes that Jesus is really for God's purpose, for God's people, and for the basic guideline in the Kingdom. Thus Jesus speaks with praise of this teacher of the law as being "not far from the kingdom of God."

The teacher of the law's question is the last of the questions asked of Jesus by religious leaders in Mark. One way or another their minds are now made up.

❑ *Mark 12:35-40.* After talking with the teacher of the law, Jesus realizes even more how different other teachers of the law can be. This difference comes to his mind as he teaches in the Temple where he sees the teachers of the law passing by. Jesus first attacks their limited understanding of God's intentions. Knowing that the teachers of the law traditionally teach that the Messiah will be the son of David, they are blind to what Scripture says about the divinity of the Messiah. He quotes Psalm 110:1 to illustrate their blindness (verse 36). Jesus notes that these teachers of the law are more interested in ceremonial impressiveness than in meeting human need. They will receive God's condemnation on the Day of Judgment.

❑ *Mark 12:41-44.* Still in the Temple, observing while teaching, Jesus sees a poor widow in the court of the women drop two coins into the offering. These copper coins were the smallest coins in value, just as our copper pennies are. Jesus sees her offering as authentic spirituality in contrast to the synthetic spirituality he had repeatedly observed in the Temple earlier. He holds her gift up as being symbolic of her total commitment.

❑ *Mark 13:1-2.* The Temple, begun about 20 B.C. and still under construction at this time, was one of the marvels of the ancient world.

❑ *Mark 13:3-37.* Andrew joins the inner circle for this conversation. Now we see a different picture of Jesus than we have met thus far in Mark. This picture of Jesus is so different that some have wondered if this story came from Mark's pen or if he used another source for this portion. Here Jesus speaks in the style of an Old Testament prophet warning of the coming day of the Lord.

Jesus warns of the destruction of the Temple, international strife, persecution and trial of his disciples, division within families, and false messiahs. Yet there are the promises of the preaching everywhere of the gospel, the enablement of the Holy Spirit, and the salvation of his own who endure. When things are at their darkest, the Son of man will come with power and light.

The "abomination that causes desolation" (verse 14) comes from Daniel 9:27 and refers to evil profaning the Temple and driving out God's servants. Again the fig tree is used as an object lesson (verses 28-29).

In studying this chapter beware of sensing a necessity to link each figure of speech to a specific historical event. The most helpful study probably is to ask, What are the overall lessons Jesus is trying to teach to disciples in all ages? His teaching is the eternal word that is much more important than completely understanding each momentary word.

DIMENSION THREE:
WHAT DOES THE BIBLE MEAN TO ME?

Mark 12:35-37—Watch Therefore

Every moment is full of meaning for Christians. We walk as those who always are watching, for we know not in what hour Christ may come. We devote ourselves to Christ's purposes, seek to copy Jesus' lifestyle, and seek to personify Christ's nature because we are those who watch. Though history turns us upside down and destroys every previous thing that we have embraced, we still know that Christ stands there—that Christ comes, that Christ will be with us *to* the end, and that he will be with us *through* the end.

On the Mount of Olives Jesus tried to say to his disciples that their future might not be the way they planned it. If they did not have something beyond the law, they might end up scared to death and shattered with insecurity. Can you give some examples of the Christian's tendency to postpone decisions? Does the word *watch* make sense only if Christ may come tomorrow?

*"My soul is overwhelmed with sorrow to the point of death,"
he said to them. "Stay here and keep watch" (14:34).*

— 12 —
The Last Mile of the Way
Mark 14

DIMENSION ONE:
WHAT DOES THE BIBLE SAY?

Answer these questions by reading Mark 14

1. What is the Jewish season? What do the Jewish religious leaders decide about Jesus? (14:1-2)

   *The Passover
   They want to arrest Him and put Him to death.*

2. What unusual act does a woman perform at the house of Simon the Leper? (14:3)

   She poured a flask of expensive perfume over His head

3. What complaint is made about her act? (14:4-5)

   Some said it was a waste, that it could have been sold and money given to the poor.

4. How does Jesus respond to the complaint? (14:6-9)

   He said to leave her alone, she was preparing His body for burial and that she would be remembered and praised

5. What does Judas Iscariot do? (14:10-11)

   He goes to the Chief priests to arrange to betray Jesus

6. What preparation do the disciples make for the Passover? (14:12-16)

7. What disturbing announcement does Jesus make at the outset of the meal? (14:17-18)

That one of them would betray Him.

8. How do the disciples react to this revelation? (14:19)

They were very sad. And asked each "Am I the one?"

9. How does Jesus identify the betrayer? (14:20-21)

It was one of them eating with Him

10. What symbolic acts does Jesus introduce at this meal? (14:22-25)

Giving the bread for His body and giving the cup of wine for His blood

11. Where do Jesus and the disciples go after the meal? (14:26)

Out to the Mount of Olives

12. What warning does Jesus give the disciples? How does Peter react? (14:27-29)

That they would all desert Him.

13. What is Jesus' prediction to Peter, and what is Peter's reaction? (14:30-31)

14. Where do they go next? (14:32) Who goes with Jesus? (14:33)

15. What is Jesus' feeling and his prayer? (14:34-36, 39, 41)

16. What are his three companions doing? (14:37-41)

They went to sleep.

17. What sudden interruption takes place? (14:42-43)

A mob appears, led by Judas

18. How is Jesus betrayed? What is Jesus' response? (14:44-49)

Judas had said to arrest the one he greets

19. What happens to the disciples? (14:50-54)

They fled.

20. What problem does the Sanhedrin have with witnesses against Jesus? (14:55-59)

21. What questions does the high priest direct to Jesus? What is Jesus' response? (14:60-62)

22. What symbolic act does the high priest perform? (14:63)

23. What decision does the Sanhedrin render? (14:64)

24. What accusations are made against Peter? (14:66-67, 69-70)

25. What is Peter's response? (14:68, 70, 71)

26. When the rooster crows, what happens to Peter? (14:72)

DIMENSION TWO:
WHAT DOES THE BIBLE MEAN?

Probably no chapter in the Bible is more filled with a variety of emotion than is Mark 14. We find here intense love and deep-seated hostility, secret conniving and open praise, close fellowship and intense loneliness, strong commitment and shameful betrayal, kisses and blows. This chapter begins with plotting and ends with weeping.

❑ *Mark 14:1-2.* The Passover and the Feast of Unleavened Bread were interrelated events. The Feast of Unleavened Bread was a seven-day observance as established by Moses (Exodus 12:1-28) to commemorate the deliverance of the Hebrews from slavery in Egypt. The Hebrews had eaten their meal in haste without time to wait for bread to rise when awaiting the Exodus. Part of that experience was when their homes had been "passed over" by the angel of death because the Hebrews placed the blood of a sacrificed lamb on their doorposts (Exodus 12:21-27). The Passover with its special meal was established to remember this deliverance with gratitude from generation to generation. The Passover meal took place on the first night of the Feast of Unleavened Bread.

Thousands of persons came to Jerusalem to celebrate the Passover. Thus the religious authorities wanted to get Jesus out of the way before all the crowds arrived lest there be a mob reaction.

❑ *Mark 14:3-9.* Simon the Leper appears nowhere else in Scripture so we do not know much about him. The anointing of Jesus with the valuable perfumed ointment was an expression of tribute and affection.

In referring to the "poor," Jesus is recalling Deuteronomy 15:11. In speaking of anointing his body "for my burial," Jesus is referring to the practice of placing spices or ointments on a body at the time of death to overcome the odors of decay. (See Mark 16:1.)

❑ *Mark 14:10-11.* The exact connection between the anointing and Judas's betrayal is not given. They seem to be related. John identifies Judas as the one who protests the "waste" of the ointment and as the treasurer of the disciples (12:4-5). Judas is to indicate to the chief priests where and when Jesus can be seized secretly and to lead them to Mark.

❑ *Mark 14:12-16.* Jesus is doing what many would be doing in anticipation of the crowds who were arriving in Jerusalem. He is making a dinner reservation for his group. Again, this plan suggests Jesus' familiarity with the city.

❑ *Mark 14:17-21.* The announcement of the betrayal brings dismay and sorrow to the disciples. The last sentence in verse 21, "It would be better for him if he had not been born," is a common figure of speech of that day.

❑ *Mark 14:22-25.* The Passover meal has several traditional religious observances. The unleavened bread and the cup of the fruit of the vine are passed to all those present as a part of these observances. These customary items Jesus forever filled with special meaning by injecting himself into them. From now on this bread was to remind Jesus' followers of his body and the cup of his blood, both given for them. The material and spiritual are blended to be an object lesson forever.

❑ *Mark 14:26.* The words of Psalm 113–118 were usually sung at the end of the Passover meal. They are part of the *Hallel*, the praise of God, from which the word *hallelujah* comes. To find privacy, perhaps in the olive grove of their hosts, Jesus and the disciples go to the Mount of Olives.

❑ *Mark 14:27-31.* Jesus here quotes Zechariah 13:7 about the shepherd. Jesus promises that he will still go back home to Galilee with the disciples. By promising they will not deny him, they mean they will not refuse to recognize him or ignore him.

❑ *Mark 14:32-42.* Gethsemane, meaning "oil press," was a place on the Mount of Olives. The distress appearing in verses 33-34 is far more than sadness or fear. This distress is emotional agony so severe that it could bring about death. Jesus' struggle to give himself unreservedly to God's purpose for him is that intense. *Abba* is an Aramaic word for *father*. The word *watch* carries the meaning of stay awake and observe what happens. But the three disciples are not successful.

❑ *Mark 14:43-50.* The mention of the "elders" indicates that the Jewish Council (Sanhedrin) or its officers have agreed to this mission. These were not soldiers in the customary sense who invade the olive grove but a crowd of slaves and others hired by the chief priests (verse 47). Judas indicates in the dark which person is Jesus by going to him and kissing him, calling

Jesus by the esteemed title, "Rabbi." Verse 50 is one of the saddest verses in the Gospel.

❏ **Mark 14:51-52.** The report of this unknown "young man" appears only in Mark. The story suggests that someone got up in the middle of the night with only bedclothes on to come to the garden. Apparently thought to be a disciple, he is seized and flees. Many people think this story appears here because the young man is Mark himself.

❏ **Mark 14:53-65.** This hearing takes place before the Sanhedrin. The high priest presides. Since no one would appear against Jesus, witnesses are hired but their stories do not agree. In verses 57-58 they report a complete misunderstanding of what Jesus said in 13:2. Frustrated by his inability to get evidence against Jesus, the high priest asks Jesus directly if he is the Messiah. As soon as Jesus confirms this, the high priest tears his garments, a traditional symbol of having heard blasphemy. The Sanhedrin finds Jesus "worthy of death" that only the Roman ruler can authorize.

❏ **Mark 14:66-72.** Reread verse 54. Peter impulsively follows Jesus after his arrest and ends up among the servants of the priests. One servant recognizes Peter, but Peter denies that he knows Jesus. She persuades others that Peter is a disciple. His Galilean dialect suggests he is from the same area as Jesus. As Peter resorts to profanity to convince them, the rooster crows twice, and Peter remembers Jesus' words (verses 27-31).

DIMENSION THREE:
WHAT DOES THE BIBLE MEAN TO ME?

Awareness of Neighbors' Bitter Struggles

The atmosphere in this chapter is that of contrasts. So peaceful was the setting in the garden that the disciples could fall asleep under its silent influence. How strange that their sleep is broken by the footfalls of betrayal though not disturbed by the agony of their closest friend. They are able to sleep while Jesus, to whom they had committed themselves and with whom they had dined in close intimacy and inspiring fellowship, goes through the dark night of the soul. Jesus agonizes over what is to come until he comes to a meeting of his own spirit with an unreserved commitment to God's purpose for him. How often we never know of the agony of the soul of the person who lives beside us or walks beside us! How close we can be to some people and how distant to them in their hour of greatest need! How often only crisis or agony for ourselves wakes us up!

Which is the greater sin—to be aggressively abusive or silently indifferent while Christ hurts and God waits?

"Don't be alarmed," he said. "You are looking for Jesus the Nazarene, who was crucified. He has risen! He is not here" (16:6).

— 13 —

From Darkness to Light
Mark 15–16:8

DIMENSION ONE:
WHAT DOES THE BIBLE SAY?

Answer these questions by reading Mark 15:1-20

1. Where is Jesus taken? (15:1)

   to Pilate, the Roman governor.

2. What questions does Pilate ask of Jesus? What is Jesus' response? (15:2-5)

   Pilate asked Him, "Are you the King of the Jews?"
   "Yes, it is as you say." said Jesus, but He said no more.

3. What custom does Pilate use as an attempt to free Jesus? (15:6-10)

   To release one Jewish prisoner each year at Passover time — any prisoner the people requested

4. How does the crowd respond to the offer? (15:11)

   The chief priests incited

5. What then does Pilate ask the people? How do they respond? (15:12-14)

6. What do the soldiers do? (15:16-20)

Answer these questions by reading Mark 15:21-41

7. What happens to the passerby? (15:21)

8. At the site of the Crucifixion, what happens first? (15:22-24)

9. What time is Jesus crucified? (15:25)

10. What is the written charge against Jesus? (15:26)

11. Who were crucified at the same time as Jesus? (15:27)

Two robbers

12. What jeering comments were shouted at Jesus? (15:29-32)

13. What happens at the sixth and ninth hours? (15:33-34)

14. What do bystanders do? (15:35-36)

15. What happens at the end? (15:37-39)

16. Who else is witnessing what is taking place? (15:40-41)

Answer these questions by reading Mark 15:42–16:8

17. Who is Joseph of Arimathea? (15:42-43)

18. What courageous deed does Joseph perform? (15:44-46)

19. What action do the women take? (15:47–16:2)

20. En route, what concern do they have? (16:3)

They wondered how they could roll the great stone away

21. As they enter the tomb, whom do they meet? (16:5)

A young man dressed in white (An angel)

22. What does the messenger tell them? (16:6-7)

A young man dressed in white (an angel)

23. What is the reaction of the women? (16:8)

They were very afraid

DIMENSION TWO:
WHAT DOES THE BIBLE MEAN?

In his poem entitled "Ash Wednesday," T. S. Eliot writes picturesque words to describe the feelings that Lent brings to him—a tension between death and birth. These words also describe the mood of these two chapters in Mark. The prolonged processes that, slowly but surely, have led to the dying of Jesus reach their somber climax. The dreams seem dashed upon the rocks of hopelessness. But birth leads not simply to death. The Gospel of Mark teaches us that death can lead to birth—for Jesus and his church!

❑ *Mark 15:1-5.* The Council (Sanhedrin) having decided that Jesus deserved the death sentence, consult together to determine the next step. Whatever is done must be done before the sabbath begins that evening. An early morning hearing before Pontius Pilate is arranged. Only the Romans can issue a death sentence. Pilate is the Roman administrator (procurator) of Judea. For someone to be called a king might suggest the possibility of a rebellion brewing or of treason being planned. So Pilate concentrates on that charge. Jesus' answer (verse 2) is puzzling and difficult to translate. You may wish to read several translations to see the different possibilities. The "many things" of which the chief priests accuse Jesus probably include blasphemy and threatening to destroy the Temple. Pilate's attitude of wonder can also be translated "marveled" (surprised or puzzled).

❑ *Mark 15:6-11.* The custom of releasing a prisoner may have been related to the Passover celebration of the deliverance of the Jews from bondage. Setting a prisoner free would be a form of celebrating that deliverance. We know nothing of Barabbas beyond what is stated in verse 7. Pilate expects the crowd to ask for Jesus' release, since he senses that jealousy and resentment by the religious leaders are really behind the charges. But the priests have arranged for persons in the crowd to call for Barabbas's release.

❑ *Mark 15:12-15.* Pilate continues to refer to Jesus as "the king of the Jews." He focuses on that concept, for better or for worse. Pilate completely misunderstands that Jesus never used this title; rather, his accusers did. *Crucify* comes from the Latin word for "cross" (*crux*). Crucifixion was a form of death the Romans used for rebels and disobedient slaves. Pilate was under orders by Rome to keep things peaceful in his province and to avoid rebellions. Thus, when he senses the mood of this crowd, Pilate tries to pacify them. First he does so by having Jesus beaten with a rod ("flogged" verse 15). Then, when beating Jesus is not enough, Pilate allows Jesus to be crucified.

❑ *Mark 15:16-20.* The soldiers pick up on the charge that had drawn Pilate's attention—Jesus making himself a king. In a mood of revelry they make fun of his kingship, creating a royal robe ("purple robe," verse 17), a crown ("of thorns," verse 17), and a scepter ("a staff," verse 19). They salute Jesus in mockery, kneeling with false homage. The soldiers also physically abuse Jesus as they strike him and spit on him.

❑ *Mark 15:21.* This Simon is different from any other Simon mentioned in the Bible. Cyrene is a town in North Africa that had a Jewish community. Simon would have been en route to Jerusalem for the Passover feast. Roman officials could order non-Romans to perform required services. Jesus, as part of his punishment and humiliation, is required to carry the crossbeam to the crucifixion site. He may have collapsed on the way due to loss of blood and fatigue. Simon is forced to carry the crossbeam the rest of the way.

We know nothing of Alexander. Later there was a devout Christian in the church at Rome named Rufus (Romans 16:13). This person may have been Simon's son.

❑ *Mark 15:22-26. Golgotha* means "skull," probably a skull-shaped hill outside the old city wall. Wine mixed with myrrh would be a sedative, but Jesus refuses it. The gambling for his garments fulfills a description in Psalm 22:18. The "third hour" would be 9 A.M. Either on or near the cross the charge that resulted in execution would be placed by the Romans. Interestingly, Pilate chooses again the charge of self-pronounced kingship.

❑ *Mark 15:27-32.* Two others along with Jesus were crucified, both of them robbers. The charge by the mockers in verse 29 is based on the testimony of the false witnesses in 14:57-58, who in turn had misreported what Jesus actually said about the Temple in 13:2. The "king" accusation also reappears (verse 32).

❑ *Mark 15:37-39.* The curtain of the Temple divided the Holy of Holies, where only the high priest could go once a year, from the rest of the Temple. The splitting of the curtain may symbolize an openness to God's presence to everyone through Christ's death. Or it may symbolize God's judgment on the Temple because of Christ's death. The centurion is a Roman soldier, probably commanding the soldiers who carried out the Crucifixion.

❑ *Mark 15:40-41.* These women are not mentioned elsewhere in Mark. They are introduced here because of their role after Jesus' death (16:1).

❑ *Mark 15:42-46.* Sabbath begins at sundown. Only a few hours remained in which the body could be buried. Otherwise it must remain unburied until after the sabbath. Joseph of Arimathea is a member of the Sanhedrin and a genuine servant of God's kingdom. The fact that Joseph has his own tomb above ground suggests he is a man of prominence and means.

❑ *Mark 15:47–16:4.* Since the body of Jesus had been hurriedly buried without anointing, at the first daylight opportunity after the sabbath the women go to carry out this task. The day after the sabbath would be Sunday morning or the first day of the Jewish week. A huge stone served as a protective seal for the tomb.

❑ *Mark 16:5-8.* The "white robe" suggests that the young man is an angel. The women are "dumbfounded" (*The Revised English Bible*). The messenger speaks of Jesus of Nazareth and tells them that Jesus "is going ahead of you into Galilee." Nazareth was in Galilee. There they will see Jesus. Jesus singles out Peter (verse 7) to receive the message. Remember Peter's condition in 14:72. This word is a messenger of hope and caring for Peter, as well as to all Jesus' followers.

❑ *Special Note.* The earliest and most reliable manuscripts of Mark end with verse 8. Later manuscripts have different endings that are found in various translations. These endings add some of the resurrection appearances of Jesus to the account, for none of these seem to have been in Mark's original account.

DIMENSION THREE:
WHAT DOES THE BIBLE MEAN TO ME?

What Are New Discoveries of the Truth?

At the beginning Mark gave us the theme of his account: "The beginning of the gospel about Jesus Christ, the Son of God" (1:1). At the end we read, "Trembling and bewildered, the women went out and fled from the tomb. They said nothing to anyone, because they were afraid" (16:8). Why this feeling? It was even more than the announcement of Jesus' resurrection . It was the even greater discovery of the truth of Mark's theme. They had been indeed witnesses to "the beginning of the gospel about Jesus Christ, the Son of God."

In conclusion, let me offer a passage I wrote for *Adult Bible Studies* (December–February, 1982–83, pages 92-94) that has relevance here:

In Mark's account, the stranger at the grave gives this additional information to the women: "He is going before you to Galilee; there you will see him" (16:7). . . . John tells of a meeting with Christ by the seaside (Chapter 21). And Luke ends his narrative with Christ accompanying the disciples to Bethany.

The disciples were still looking for Jesus in the old places, but he was moving into new areas. The messengers at the tomb were in effect saying this to Jesus' disciples, who came looking for his body in the customary place:

"He has outdistanced your sentiments, which led you to think he would be here. He has outdistanced your religious concepts about him. He has outdistanced your attempt to imprison him in any kind of tomb. He has gone before you. You must move out beyond your present morbid state. Go out beyond your present lifestyle. Go out beyond your preconditioned expectations of where Jesus is to be found. Go out beyond any building you would construct or any fence you would erect to pen him in, and there you will find him!"

This statement describes what Mark is all about!

Taking account of what you have learned from Mark, can you accept Jesus' new truth? What changes might you need to make in your lifestyle to experience this new truth?